Symphonies

Recent Researches in Music

A-R Editions publishes seven series of critical editions, spanning the history of Western music, American music, and oral traditions.

Recent Researches in the Music of the Middle Ages and Early Renaissance
Charles M. Atkinson, general editor

Recent Researches in the Music of the Renaissance
James Haar, general editor

Recent Researches in the Music of the Baroque Era
Christoph Wolff, general editor

Recent Researches in the Music of the Classical Era
Eugene K. Wolf†, general editor

Recent Researches in the Music of the Nineteenth and Early Twentieth Centuries
Rufus Hallmark, general editor

Recent Researches in American Music
John M. Graziano, general editor

Recent Researches in the Oral Traditions of Music
Philip V. Bohlman, general editor

Each edition in *Recent Researches* is devoted to works by a single composer or to a single genre. The content is chosen for its high quality and historical importance and is edited according to the scholarly standards that govern the making of all reliable editions.

For information on establishing a standing order to any of our series, or for editorial guidelines on submitting proposals, please contact:

A-R Editions, Inc.
Middleton, Wisconsin

800 736-0070 (U.S. book orders)
608 836-9000 (phone)
608 831-8200 (fax)
http://www.areditions.com

Recent Researches in the Music of the Nineteenth and Early Twentieth Centuries, 38

Alice Mary Smith

Symphonies

Edited by Ian Graham-Jones

A-R Editions, Inc.
Middleton, Wisconsin

A-R Editions, Inc., Middleton, Wisconsin
© 2003 by A-R Editions, Inc.

All rights reserved. No part of this book may be reproduced or transmitted in any form by any electronic or mechanical means (including photocopying, recording, or information storage and retrieval) without permission in writing from the publisher.

The purchase of this edition does not convey the right to perform it in public, nor to make a recording of it for any purpose. Such permission must be obtained in advance from the publisher.

A-R Editions is pleased to support scholars and performers in their use of *Recent Researches* material for study or performance. Subscribers to any of the *Recent Researches* series, as well as patrons of subscribing institutions, are invited to apply for information about our "Copyright Sharing Policy."

Printed in the United States of America

ISBN 0-89579-550-7
ISSN 0193-5364

∞ The paper used in this publication meets the minimum requirements of the American National Standard for Information Sciences—Permanence of Paper for Printed Library Materials, ANSI Z39.48-1984.

Contents

Acknowledgments   vi

Introduction   vii
  The Composer   vii
  The Music   ix
  Notes   xi

Plates   xiii

Symphony in C Minor (1863)
    I. Grave; Allegro ma non troppo   3
   II. Allegretto amorevole   72
  III. Allegro ma non troppo   89
  IV. Allegro maestoso   121

Symphony in A Minor (1876)
    I. Allegro   187
   II. Andante   239
  III. Minuetto: Allegretto   269
  IV. Allegro   277

Critical Report   345
  Sources   345
  Editorial Methods   345
  Critical Notes   346
  Note   349

Acknowledgments

These works are now published by permission of the Royal Academy of Music. My thanks go to Heather Harrison for making available the Alice Mary Smith manuscripts to the present editor; to the West Sussex Record Office for their assistance with the A. H. M. Kempe papers; to the Royal Academy of Music library for their help with references and for making available the donated material; to Jürgen Schaarwächter for his assistance in providing a background list of nineteenth-century British symphonies; and to Oliver Davies, Keeper, Department of Portraits and Performance History at the Royal College of Music, for locating references in nineteenth-century journals.

Introduction

The Composer

At a time when women composers were starting to write in one of the most popular genres of Victorian England, the drawing room song, Alice Mary Smith (1839–84) was almost certainly the first woman composer to consistently write larger-scale chamber, choral, and orchestral works. She was certainly the first in Britain to have written and to have had performed a symphony, the Symphony in C Minor of 1863.[1] The Royal Academy of Music, founded in 1822 and situated in Tenterden Street, Hanover Square, London, accepted a number of women students, and its first woman professor of harmony, Kate Loder (1825–1904) had composed an overture and string quartets in the 1840s.[2] The only other woman to have composed a symphony in Alice Mary Smith's lifetime was Oliveria Prescott (1842–1919), whose *Alkestis* Symphony (presumed lost) was written for the Alexandra Palace symphonic competition for British composers held in 1876, as was Smith's second symphony in A minor.

Alice Mary Smith was born in London on 19 May 1839, the third child of Richard Smith and Elizabeth Lumley.[3] Her father, a wealthy lace merchant, had a London house at 57 Guildford (now Guilford) Street, Russell Square, as well as a country address of The Lodge, Littlehampton, on the Sussex coast. Her elder brothers trained in the law and, after her untimely death at the age of forty-five, both became eminent in the profession. Richard Horton-Smith (b. 1831) was elected to the bar in 1859, became a Queen's Counsel in 1877, and held the position of director (i.e., a senior member of the governing board) of the Royal Academy of Music from 1886, being elected vice-president of that institution in 1916. He later became honorary counsel to the Philharmonic Society. Lumley Smith (b. 1834) became a judge of the County Court in 1892, as did Alice Mary Smith's husband in the following year.[4] Her husband's obituary in *The Times* mentions that Alice Mary Smith was "the elder daughter of Richard Smith," but no details of a younger sister have been found.

Known in the family as Mary,[5] she studied music for a while with William Sterndale Bennett, who became principal of the Royal Academy of Music in 1866, and then chiefly with George Alexander Macfarren, who assumed the principalship of the R.A.M. in 1875 and who took a keen interest in his pupil's music throughout her composing years. Her music first came to public notice with the publication by Leader and Cock of "Weep no more!" in 1859, a canzonet to words by John Fletcher, as can be seen from the review in *The Spectator* (5 March):

> Weep no more! . . . gives promise of remarkable talent. The melody is flowing, expressive, and quite in the spirit of the fine verse of our old English dramatist; and the accompaniment is in the chaste, simple style which we should expect from a scholar of her master [i.e., Macfarren].

Her first substantial instrumental composition, the Piano Quartet No. 1 in B-flat Major, was played by The Musical Society of London, an organization whose aim was to give the members the opportunity to try out their music, in March 1861. The notice in *The Musical World* of 23 March of that year states:

> The first trial of new chamber compositions took place at the Marylebone Institution on Wednesday evening, when the following pieces were played: Trio in G minor (M.S.), pianoforte, violin, violoncello (S. W. Waley, F.); sonata in G (M.S.), pianoforte (E. Aguilar, F.);[6] sonata in A minor (M.S.) pianoforte and violin (A. Ries, A.); quartet in B flat (M.S.), pianoforte, violin, viola, violoncello (Alice M. Smith, L.A.).[7]
>
> While all the above compositions were praised for their classical feeling and structure, Mr. Aguilar's sonata—played by himself—found special admirers, and Miss Alice M. Smith's quartet created evident surprise. This young lady is a pupil of Mr. Macfarren's, and betokens unusual ability, for one of her sex, in the highest school of writing. The trials of new compositions given by the society are worthy [of] the attention of all composers, and should be noted by them emphatically.

In the following year her second string quartet in D major was performed, but it was with her Symphony in C Minor, again tried by The Musical Society of London at the Hanover Square Rooms,[8] that represented the turning point in her career. This was clearly an important meeting, being held on the anniversary of Mendelssohn's death, the symphony being conducted by Frank Mori.[9] The programme was:

Symphony in C minor, No. 1	Alice Mary Smith
Concerto for violin in E major	Henry Baumer
Overture "Cynthia's revels"	Charles Donald Macleane [*sic*]
Symphony in A minor	John Francis Barnett
Fantasia for pianoforte and orchestra	Henry Charles Banister
Overture	Jas. Lea Summers.[10]

vii

The *Illustrated London News* of 14 November 1863 reports:

> On the same evening, at the Hanover-square Rooms, the Musical Society of London had a trial-performance of new orchestral compositions by members of the society. Several symphonies and overtures were performed by a full and excellent orchestra, which did them every justice. Amongst the most remarkable was a symphony in C minor by Miss Alice Mary Smith and a symphony in A minor by Mr. John Francis Barnett,[11] both admirable compositions, which did honour to the talents of their authors. Miss Smith's symphony especially, coming from the pen of a young lady, was a striking proof of the sound studies and high attainments of the female votaries of the art in this country. We trust that these symphonies will be brought before the public in the course of the ensuing season.

A report in *The Orchestra* of 27 February 1864 of a later meeting of The Musical Society of London, where the programme started with "Overture in E (Endymion) Alice Mary Smith, L.A.," and which also included a flute concerto by Macfarren, states:

> There were on Wednesday six orchestral aspirants, of whom one is a lady, already favourably known by the production of other important works. On a former trial night, this lady, Miss A. M. Smith, distinguished herself by the production of a symphony which promised much for her future success. On the present occasion Miss Smith produced an overture on the myth of "Endymion."

Not all of her reviews, however, were positive. *The Graphic* (25 November 1871) says of her second *Endymion* Overture (1869): "In brief, the lady composer essayed a task beyond her strength, and, though largely availing herself of what had been done by others, the result is *nil*."

Other major works followed, including two piano quartets; an operetta *Gisela of Rüdesheim*,[12] performed by the Fitzwilliam Musical Society, Cambridge; her third concert overture *Lalla Rookh* (on an epic poem by Thomas Moore); an Introduction and Allegro in C Minor for piano and orchestra; and *The Masque of Pandora*, a large-scale dramatic work for soloists and orchestra in eight movements.[13] This was to have been her last major composition for a while, for on 2 January 1867 Alice Mary Smith married Frederick Meadows White (1829–98), a barrister of the Inner Temple and later QC,[14] after which she moved from her parents' home to a prestigious address close to Hyde Park, 42 Sussex Gardens. In November of that year she was elected Female Professional Associate of the Philharmonic Society.

Apart from the fourth piano quartet in G minor, the period immediately following her marriage appears to have produced no major compositions, as Mrs. Meadows White (as she was now known) was concerned with raising a family, the couple having two daughters, Ida (known as Gay, who became an extravagant socializer in later life) and Hilda.[15] While it was considered the primary duty of the wife in Victorian society to be responsible for the management of the household affairs, her husband, a keen amateur musician, gave every encouragement to Mary to promote her talents.[16] In 1887, shortly after her death, he was appointed a director (i.e., a senior governor of the board) of the Royal Academy of Music, he became a founding member of the examining body The Associated Board of the Royal Academy of Music and the Royal College of Music (now the Associated Board of the Royal Schools of Music),[17] and was also standing counsel to the Philharmonic Society. He attended lectures at the Royal Institution and the Royal Musical Association, which were only open to elected members, and was regularly seen at major London concerts. His wife's own connection with the Royal Academy of Music was maintained, and by 1880 she had become a life member of that institution, subscribing £50—a not insubstantial sum, few other subscribers having given more.[18]

The two years 1869–70 saw her writing three new major works. In 1869 she re-wrote her overture *Endymion*, with much new material, in the same key of E major,[19] as well as composing a number of songs, an Intermezzo for piano, and Melody and Scherzo for cello and piano. The following year saw two new chamber music works, a string quartet in A major,[20] performed by the New Philharmonic Society (being the opening item of the second Soirée Musicale of the season), and the Clarinet Sonata in A Major, performed with the same society by the clarinettist Henry Lazarus,[21] with the composer at the piano. The difficulty of the piano part in this work is evidence of the composer's ability as a pianist.[22] Although *New Grove 2* and *The New Grove Dictionary of Women Composers* list a clarinet concerto, which is also mentioned in some obituary notices, there is no evidence of such a work. Only the slow movement of the clarinet sonata, orchestrated by the composer, exists, having three performances in 1872–73 at the Norwich and Brighton Festivals and in London.[23] In 1876 she responded to the Alexandra Palace competition for symphonies by British composers, resulting in her second symphony in A minor, but it was not completed in time and thus not submitted.

From 1879 she resumed an uninterrupted active period of composing and attending performances of her latest works. A new overture, *Jason, or The Argonauts and the Sirens*, scored for a particularly full orchestra including piccolo, four horns, and ophicleide, was hurriedly composed, judging by the hastily written manuscript. Performances of this work were invited by Wilhelm Ganz,[24] conductor of the New Philharmonic Society's concerts, and for August Manns's Crystal Palace Saturday concerts.[25] Her works began to be performed regularly at these concerts and in 1882 she was chosen to make a presentation to Manns. Sir George Macfarren, as chairman, spoke, seconded by George Grove,[26] and "to Mrs. Meadows White fell the pleasing duty of handing to Mr. Manns a purse containing 700 guineas and a handsome album, in which 494 contributors had inscribed their names."

Other large-scale works for choir and orchestra followed: *Ode to the North-East Wind*, a cantata for choir and orchestra, was performed by the Hackney Choral Society conducted by the eminent musician of the time,

Ebenezer Prout;[27] the ode *The Passions,* performed at the Three Choirs Festival at Hereford in 1882 and by the Bradford Choral Society the following year; two works for male voices, *Song of the Little Baltung* (1883), and her last complete work, *The Red King* (1884). All these choral works were published by Novello and Co., the *Ode to the North-East Wind* appearing to have been the most popular, having sold over 1000 copies in each of the years 1885 and 1886. These works continued to be performed until the turn of the century.

In April 1883 Mrs. Meadows White was elected an honorary member of the Royal Academy of Music (Hon. R.A.M.), an award given only to distinguished musicians. Later that year continuing throat problems had worsened and she travelled to Aix-les-Bains in France to see a specialist for laryngitis. Her last incomplete work was a setting of *The Valley of Remorse,* the words from a poem by a Miss Bevington. On 4 December 1884 she died of typhoid fever at the age of forty-five.

Such was her fame in America that *The New York Times* carried a column obituary. Only short obituary notices, however, appeared in the British national press, *The Times* commenting on her lack of originality: ". . . she published several compositions, not, perhaps, marked by very striking originality, but all of them refined in style and well written. She was among the few female composers who attempted the higher forms of choral and orchestral music." Ebenezer Prout's obituary in *The Atheneum*, quoted in part in *The New Grove Dictionary of Women Composers*, stating that "her sympathies were evidently with the classic rather than with the romantic school," produced a comment from her husband, to which Prout replied in a letter:

> I think . . . that you have understood to imply more than I really meant when I spoke of Mrs. White's sympathies being with the classical rather than the romantic school. I meant *in her own style of composition,* and had not [any] idea of suggesting that her sympathies were limited. I should write just in the same way with regard to myself. I believe I admire Wagner and the best works of the modern school as much as anyone can do; but when I write I believe my music shows absolutely no trace of their influence, but is founded more on the style of the old masters; and this was all that I meant in the remark I made. I can admire what it would not be in my nature to try to imitate; and I believe it was the same with Mrs. White.
>
> Believe me, my dear Mr. White, Yours very sincerely, Ebenezer Prout.[28]

There exists little information on her personality, but an article appearing in the *Boston Evening Traveller* of 12 March 1885 gives an interesting account of a friendship:[29]

> Another, not so recent, but equally sad death, is that of a most distinguished and gifted woman, Mrs. Meadows White of London. Her great reputation as a musical composer has reached America. It is she who wrote the music to Longfellow's "Masque of Pandora," and who was the first, perhaps the only woman composer of eminence, of classical, concerted music. She is known to us as the author of delicious songs, under her maiden name of "Alice Mary Smith," and as the author of the popular duet "Maying," arranged for tenor and soprano voices, and so often sung at our concerts. She is known in England as the first of creative musical artists, the only one who has written for the orchestra, both alone, and in combination with voices. I met her at Aix-les-Bains, where she went to consult the distinguished Doctor Brachet for chronic laryngitis, from which she was a sufferer.
>
> I was attracted by the gifted woman before I knew who she was, by her quiet, concentrated air of power, and in a three weeks' sojourn together amid those delightful mountains we grew to be almost friends. I had many talks with her on the subject, dear to both of us, of woman's work in those fields, generally supposed to belong exclusively to men. There was a delicacy and a modesty, very personal and very charming about this highly gifted creature that endeared her to everyone. She seemed to be carrying about her genius, as a trust, and a sacred one. She was like one of Raphael's sybils, wrapped in heavenly contemplation, a beloved and happy wife and mother, she seemed to need only health to be perfectly happy. She had conquered much, but she wore the laurels meekly. An account of her compositions, cantatas, overtures, and concertos performed at the Musical Society of London, the New Philharmonic Society, the Crystal Palace Saturday concerts, the Liverpool Philharmonic Society, the Hereford Festival, etc., etc., would fill a volume.
>
> She had the highest artistic culture, the most refined poetic feeling, and the most original mind. I heard of her lamented death early in the month of December, and although I have already written of her, I desire once again to record my respect and grief for her. In the music loving city of Boston—that modern Weimar, where genius is worshipped—at one of your Philharmonic societies, should be played her cantata, written to illustrate Collins's "Ode the Passions," also her "Masque of Pandora," and her cantata on Kingsley's song of the "Little Baltung." Hoping, as I did, to meet her in London, and later in America—toward whose shores her prophetic soul turned as the hopeful home of a new school of music, I was deeply grieved to hear of her death, and I lay my humble leaflet on the early grave of this daughter of song and melody.

The Girl's Own Paper (31 January 1885) gives an extensive obituary as well as an etching of the composer, and concludes: "Mrs. White's society was much courted by her friends on account of her great charm of manner and vivaciousness of disposition. . . . Devoted to her art, Mrs. Smith was alike free from affectation and conceit; and in the roll of female musicians her name will hold an honourable place."[30]

The Music

Walter Macfarren, brother of Alice Mary Smith's teacher, writes in an article of 1886 entitled "Women's Work in Music":[31]

> In the highest branches of musical composition it can hardly be affirmed that women have reached the loftiest standard. No great oratorio nor successful opera occurs to the mind as having resulted from feminine productiveness. On the other hand, however, who shall say that the sex which has given us an Alice Mary Smith (Mrs. Meadows White), a Charlotte Helen Sainton-Dolby, an Agnes Zimmerman, and a Maude

Valérie White, has done nothing to enrich the stores of musical literature? The first two named and deeply-lamented ladies have left evidence of their ambition to essay music composition in some of its more elevated forms,[32] and the ample recognition of these attempts have received at the hands of the public is the truest testimony of their success. Mrs. Meadows White produced and published more compositions than we can enumerate, but some of her works are too good and too important to leave uncited.

He later goes on to mention Mrs. Mounsey Bartholomew and Oliveria Prescott, "whose highly-meritorious symphony,[33] overtures and other compositions, vocal and instrumental, might be with advantage more frequently heard." The importance he attaches to Alice Mary Smith's major works is significant and her two symphonies, the second of which received no performances, are good examples of the orchestral music that was coming from the pen of many composers in England in that period.

The principal English symphonists in the three decades before Smith's C-minor symphony were Cipriani Potter (first principal of the R.A.M.), whose nine symphonies were composed between 1819 and 1834; William Sterndale Bennett, who wrote four youthful symphonies between 1832 and 1836; and the prolific workaholic George Alexander Macfarren, who had written eight symphonies before 1845. All these works may best be summarized as being post-Beethoven in style, with a strong influence of Mendelssohn, and firmly based on classical principles in both the instrumentation and the techniques of orchestration. The use of four horns is relatively uncommon in English symphonies in this period, although a choir of three trombones may be found in Potter's last two symphonies. Only a handful of symphonies were written by minor British composers prior to Smith's first symphony in 1863, by names such as Henry Charles Banister (four youthful symphonies, his last written in 1853)[34] and Emanuel A. Aguilar (three symphonies, his third in 1854)—both composers mentioned in reviews quoted above. John Lodge Ellerton's six symphonies should also be noted (his last two in 1858 use four horns and three trombones), and also Joseph Street's two symphonies (both without trombones), the first of which appeared in 1857. It is significant that none of these works appear to explore some of the more advanced styles of the continental composers, nearly all being in the traditional four movements and using classical structures. Programmatic titles, however, were not uncommon in English symphonies. Ellerton's "Waldsymphonie," no. 3 (1857); Sullivan's "Irish" (1866); Alfred Holmes's "The Siege of Paris" and "Robin Hood"; and Oliveria Prescott's "Alkestis" symphony mentioned above are the only known titled symphonies prior to 1876. Smith's symphonies, however, are totally free from programmatic overtones, unlike her six concert overtures, all of which are based on narrative poems or mythological subjects.

It must be noted that, of the continental orchestral music popular in Britain by the 1860s, Beethoven, Spohr, and Mendelssohn featured most heavily in concert programmes of the time. Schubert's symphonies were almost totally unknown, and the Schumann symphonies were rarely heard, nos. 1 and 3 being played once each in London, in 1853 and 1856.

It is within this traditional background that the first Smith symphony appeared, and it is in this context that this work must be assessed. She had been studying with Macfarren, who became blind by the 1860s, for some while previously. Smith's first work shows the sound techniques in orchestration of her teachers. Both her symphonies use two natural horns, though her overture *Jason* uses four (two each in different keys), with more adventurous horn writing. Typical Mendelssohnian soloistic horn passages are found notably in the C-minor work as, for example, in the first movement, measures 174–93 and 484–503, and the opening of the scherzo. The three trombones are effectively used in chorus, both in climactic passages and in places where they are tellingly used *piano*, most notably in the third movement. An unusual feature is the occasional use of the bass trombone solo to emphasize a phrase (see the first movement, mm. 359–61). Her use of solo woodwind is particularly effective. The bassoon is given solo prominence, as in the horn passages of the C-minor symphony mentioned above; the clarinet is used throughout its register (note the use of its lowest register in doubling the violin melody an octave lower in the second movement, mm. 100–106), as well as showing its agility in decorative scale passages such as in the scherzo, measures 220–22. Though one senses that the oboe was not perhaps her most favorite of instruments, she sometimes gives passages of unaccompanied solos to the instrument, such as in measures 301–10 in the first movement, and particularly in the cadenza-like section in the fourth movement, measures 184–88. Her methods of development are traditional but effective, and her structures are always well planned, with contrasting, lyrical second subjects. The Mendelssohnian scherzo, unusually through-composed, without a separate trio and with no repeats, is particularly effective, and the rondo finale, with its brief return of the introduction to the first movement's cello theme, now given to the oboe, is typical of its models. Cello melodies, independent of the double bass, are common, the most extended example being in the second movement, measures 44–71. Violas in their highest register (extending to a top b♭") are exploited in the scherzo (see mm. 144–48). The double bass part of this symphony is written for performance on a three-stringed instrument, tuned A_1-D-G, so that where its doubling of the cello takes it below its register, it is written an octave higher. These places have been transposed editorially for performance on the standard four-stringed instrument with the low E_1 string. Three-stringed basses were the norm in Britain in the nineteenth century, so it is perhaps unusual that the composer follows the more modern practice of writing for the double bass with the added fourth string in the 1876 symphony.

The second symphony in A minor, written in response to the Alexandra Palace competition, was not submitted in time, and the finale appears to have been hastily composed, with numerous alterations and omissions of detail in the score. It may be that her intention was to prepare a fair copy for her competition entry. The work is unsigned, the title cover headed: "Symphony in A minor By Σ," the Greek letter sigma presumably being the pseudonym chosen for her entry to the competition. On the front cover her husband has written: "A. M. W. Written for, but not sent in in time, & so did not compete for the prize offered for a symphony by the Alex^ra Palace C^n," which he dated 13 January 1885 (see under "Sources" for full detail). The notice of the competition in *The Musical Times* of February 1876 reads:

> The authorities of the Alexandra Palace offer two prizes of £20 and £5 respectively, together with a certificate, for the best two Orchestral Symphonies to be written by British composers, the judges being Professor C. A. Macfarren and Herr Joachim. The work which gains the first prize is to be performed at one of the Saturday concerts, and the second, if of sufficient merit, will also be presented to the public. Manuscripts must be sent to Mr. H. Weist-Hill on or before March 13.[35]

Even allowing for the notice to have appeared two weeks earlier in *The Musical World* (a weekly publication), it gave little time for Alice Mary Smith to complete a fair copy, and one can therefore understand the hurried writing, particularly in the finale. The first prize was awarded to Macfarren's son-in-law, Francis William Davenport, for his Symphony No. 1 in D Minor; and the second to the young Charles Villiers Stanford for his first symphony in B-flat.[36] From Frederick Meadows White's note on the score of the A-minor symphony it appears that a third prize was created for Oliveria Prescott's *Alkestis* Symphony.[37] Prescott was amanuensis to Macfarren at this time, and this work is, as far as is known, the only other symphony by a British woman composer in the nineteenth century.

It is unclear whether Smith was influenced by any other symphonic works prior to 1876, but Julius Benedict's first of his two symphonies had been performed in London[38] and Macfarren had produced his last, ninth symphony in E minor, as well as Ebenezer Prout his first, in 1874. Although using the same instrumentation as the C-minor work, the orchestration seems generally more conventional, without some of the interesting touches noted in the earlier work. Its first movement shows more concise, tauter writing than the C-minor symphony, with its second subject unusually in the submediant key, and the *Andante* uses greater contrasting materials with wider-ranging modulations. Although not titled as a minuet, the composer has written "Menuetto D.C." at the end of the third movement (modernized to "Minuetto" in the edition). It follows the classical minuet and trio structure with its traditional repeats, and oboes as well as trombones are omitted in the scoring. The minuet seems somewhat tame after the effective scherzo of the C minor work, although the trio has the elegance and deftness shown in the scherzo of her A-major string quartet of 1870. The finale is another strong movement, this time in sonata form, with an extensive coda.

A third symphony in G major is listed in both *New Grove 2* and *The New Grove Dictionary of Women Composers*, but no record of this can be found by the editor. The obituary in *The Girl's Own Paper* lists her works in some detail and says: "... she has besides left in MS. a second symphony."[39] One would also have expected her husband to have mentioned its existence in his detailed list of her works prepared for her obituary, but his notes state: "Among her works which have neither been published nor performed in public are a second symphony...."[40]

Notes

1. The only other symphonies by a woman composer before this date are those of Jeanne-Louise Farrenc, whose three symphonies of 1841, 1845, and 1847 were performed in Paris.

2. Coming from an influential family of musicians, Kate Loder was a successful concert pianist as well as a composer. As Lady Thompson, the wife of an eminent surgeon, she, with Cipriani Potter (principal of the R.A.M. until 1859), gave the first British performance of Brahms's *German Requiem* with piano duet accompaniment.

3. L. G. H. Horton-Smith, *The Ancient Northern Family of Lumley* (St. Albans: Campfield Press, 1948), lists details of the Lumley family and contains a portrait of her mother, Elizabeth Lumley. (Copy from the A. H. M. Kempe mss. [Acc. 8398], held by the West Sussex Record Office, Chichester, U.K.; hereafter cited as the "Kempe papers.")

4. *The Law List* (London: Stevens) from 1893 onwards gives details of her brothers' positions. See also *Who Was Who*, vol. 2, *1916–28* (London: A. & C. Black, 1992).

5. *A Family History of the Kempes*, ed. Venetia Carse and Dorothea Hughes, vol. 2, p. 39 (copy in West Sussex Record Office). For more on the family, see note 1 appended to the critical report.

6. Brief details of the composers not listed in *The New Grove Dictionary of Music and Musicians*, either in the 1st edition (hereafter *NG1*) or the 2d (*NG2*), are given here. Simon Waley, Jewish pianist and amateur composer (b. 1827), wrote mainly chamber and piano works. Emanuel Aguilar (b. 1824), of Spanish parentage, was a skilled concert pianist who wrote three symphonies, operas, and a considerable quantity of piano and chamber music. (See *British Musical Biography* [Birmingham: J. D. Brown and S. S. Stratton, 1897].)

7. These presumably indicate the categories of membership: F. = Fellow, A. = Associate, L.A. = Lady Associate.

8. For an engraving of this concert venue, see *NG2*, s.v. "London. VI. Musical life, 1800–1945. 2. Concert life" (p. 139), by Cyril Ehrlich, Simon McVeigh, and Michael Musgrave; also

in the *NG1* article on London (under section VI, part 5, by Henry Raynor).

9. Mori (1820–73), composer and conductor, established The London Orchestra in 1854.

10. See note 6. Baumer (b. 1835), minor composer and teacher, was head of the Watford School of Music. Maclean (b. 1843) was primarily an organist who only wrote a few works. Summers (b. 1837), a blind pupil of Kate Loder and Macfarren, composed mainly a small quantity of chamber music.

11. Barnett (b. 1837); this was his only symphony, he being better known for his later cantatas and an operetta.

12. *Gisela of Rüdesheim,* for three characters and a chorus of retainers and villagers, and scored with a small orchestra, was erroneously described by her husband in a list provided for her obituary as "Rüdesheim or Gisela—cantata for soli and chorus." It is listed in *NG2* and *The New Grove Dictionary of Women Composers* under the incorrect title.

13. Based on Longfellow's poem, the work has eleven characters and a chorus. Only the Overture and two Intermezzi were fully scored and performed; the remaining movements exist in piano reduction only.

14. Barristers may be elected as Queen's Counsel only after ten years' practice at the bar. Frederick Meadows White was made a QC in 1877, became Recorder of Canterbury from 1883 to 1893, and Judge of the County Court of Clerkenwell in London from 1893, when he became His Honour Judge Meadows White. He died in 1898 of "deterioration of the brain caused by overwork." (Obituary, *The Times,* 23 May 1898.)

15. Alice Ida was born in 1868, Alice Hilda a year later.

16. In a discussion on a Royal Musical Association paper on "Woman in Relation to Musical Art," Frederick Meadows White stated that "there is nothing inconsistent with the little eminence my wife has attained in music with the good management of domestic affairs." See Sophie Fuller, *The Pandora Guide to Women Composers* (London: Pandora, an imprint of HarperCollins, 1994), 284.

17. Frederick Meadows White continued as a director of the R.A.M. and as the representative of that institution on the Associated Board until shortly before his death in 1898. The R.A.M. minutes (23 March 1891) record: "It was unanimously resolved to accord F. W. Meadows White a vote of thanks for his constant attendance at the Associated Board and for so well protecting the interests of the Academy thereat."

18. Royal Academy of Music Prospectuses, 1880–84.

19. The second *Endymion* Overture is a complete revision, being a considerably more extended work, although incorporating some material from the 1864 version.

20. This is incorrectly listed as A minor in *NG2* and in *The New Grove Dictionary of Women Composers,* although correct in Grove's first edition of *A Dictionary of Music and Musicians* (1879–89).

21. Lazarus (1815–95) was one of the most important and influential clarinettists of the time.

22. The Clarinet Sonata in A Major and the String Quartet in A Major, edited by Ian Graham-Jones, are published by Hildegard Publishing Company (Box 332, Bryn Mawr, PA 19010).

23. Her husband (maybe incorrectly) listed "Concerto for Clarinet and Orchestra: Andante: Norwich Festival 1872" in his list of works prepared for her obituary. It may well be that Smith intended to orchestrate the complete sonata, or that the outer movements are lost. It is nevertheless certain that only the Andante was performed, the separately bound full score of which is in the collection of her manuscripts.

24. Ganz, conductor of the New Philharmonic Society from 1874, encouraged performances of new works at his concerts.

25. Sir August Manns ran the Saturday afternoon concerts at popular prices at the Crystal Palace and, like Ganz, included new works by British composers.

26. Grove had contributed analytical notes for these concerts for many years, and 1879 saw the publication of the first edition of his dictionary of music.

27. There are letters in the Kempe papers in the West Sussex Record Office from Prout advising Smith on points of orchestration, on misprints in the score, and mildly chiding her for not putting dynamics into every part in the score, a characteristic feature of her manuscript symphonies (see editorial methods).

28. Kempe papers.

29. Kempe papers.

30. Kempe papers.

31. *The Clifton Chronicle and Directory,* 20 January 1886, copy from the Kempe papers.

32. Charlotte Sainton-Dolby died only a few months after Alice Mary Smith, but her only large-scale works were four cantatas for chorus and orchestra, written after 1876.

33. *British Musical Biography* lists two symphonies by Prescott, in B-flat and D minor. Prescott, although only three years younger than Smith, did not start composing seriously until 1876. The *Alkestis* Symphony was followed by a Magnificat for soloists, chorus, and full orchestra; several chamber works in the last two decades of the century; overtures; and a piano concerto. The manuscripts appear not to have survived.

34. Banister (1831–97) taught harmony at the R.A.M. from 1853.

35. The Alexandra Palace, situated in North London, announced this competition in an attempt to provide a more "up-market" image in order to compete with the successful Crystal Palace (South London) Saturday concerts. There were thirty-eight entrants for the somewhat paltry prize money. (See P. Scholes, *The Mirror of Music, 1844–1944* [London: Novello, jointly with Oxford University Press, 1947], 199–200.) Weist-Hill was musical director and organist at the Alexandra Palace.

36. Davenport (1847–1925), another pupil of Macfarren (whose daughter he married), did not follow up this success, writing few other works, unlike the prolific Stanford. Macfarren's wife, Clarina Thalia Andrae (Natalia Macfarren), was, incidentally, Robert Schumann's god-daughter. Both the Davenport and Stanford symphonies received a performance at the Alexandra Palace.

37. This is the only record found so far of an extra third prize.

38. Benedict (1804–85), a German by birth, moved to England in 1845 and conducted several orchestras.

39. See 31 January 1885, p. 276.

40. Kempe papers. Grove's first edition of *A Dictionary of Music and Musicians* (1879–89) lists two symphonies: C minor (1863) and G (18—).

Plate 1. An early photograph of Alice Mary Smith. Reproduced from the A. H. M. Kempe papers (Acc. 8398) by courtesy of Mrs. Venetia Carse, and with acknowledgments to the West Sussex Record Office and the County Archivist.

Plate 2. A later photograph of Alice Mary Meadows White. Reproduced from the A. H. M. Kempe papers (Acc. 8398) by courtesy of Mrs. Venetia Carse, and with acknowledgments to the West Sussex Record Office and the County Archivist.

Plate 3. The opening page of the full score of the Symphony in C Minor. Courtesy of the Royal Academy of Music.

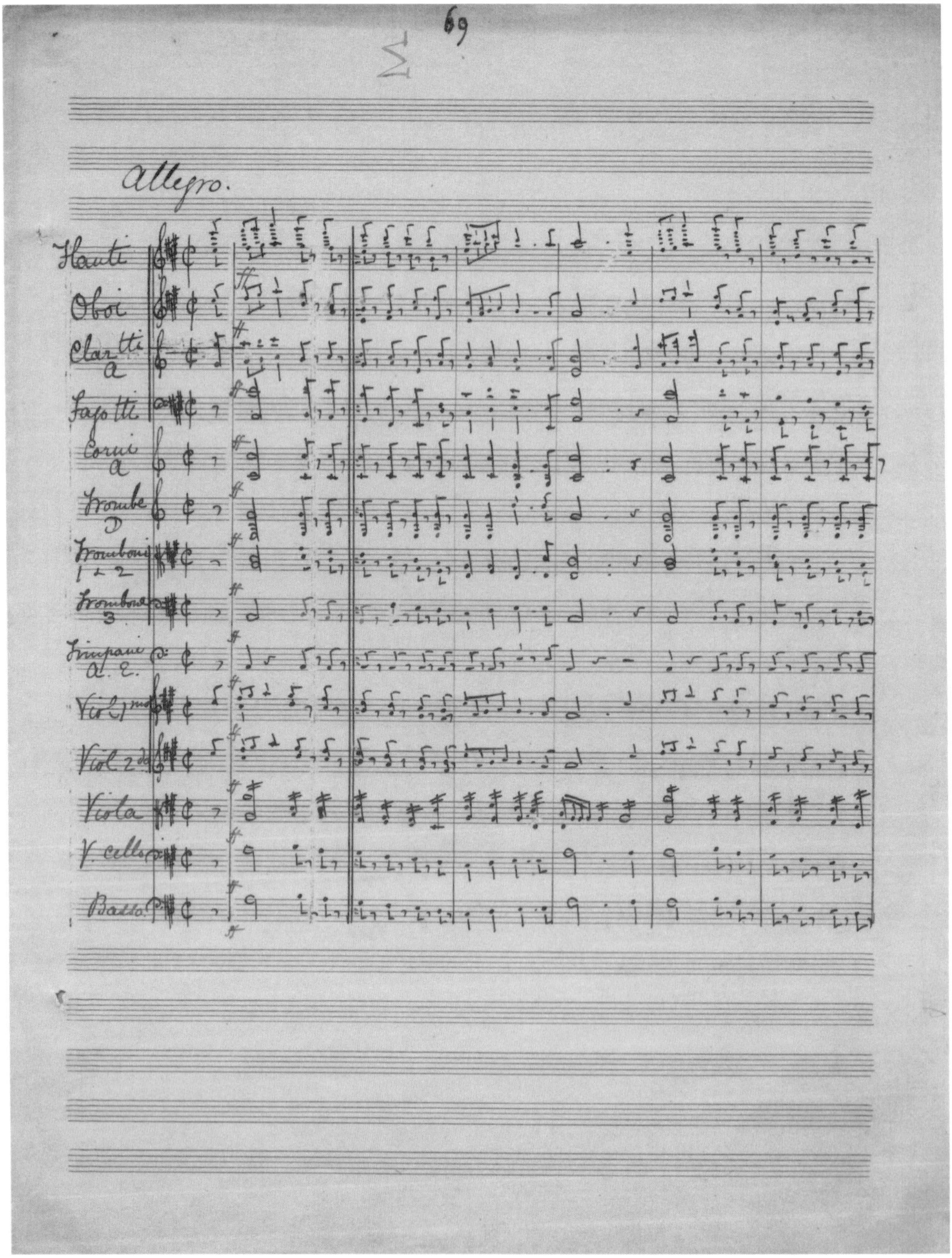

Plate 4. The first page of the fourth movement of the Symphony in A Minor. Courtesy of the Royal Academy of Music.

Plate 5. The second page of the first violin part of the Symphony in C Minor. Courtesy of the Royal Academy of Music.

Symphony in C Minor (1863)

INSTRUMENTS

Flute (Fl.) 1, 2
Oboe (Ob.) 1, 2
Clarinet (Cl.) 1, 2
Bassoon (Bn.) 1, 2

Horn (Hn.) 1, 2
Trumpet (Tpt.) 1, 2
Alto Trombone (A. Trb.)
Tenor Trombone (T. Trb.)
Bass Trombone (B. Trb.)

Timpani (Timp.)

Violin (Vn.) 1
Violin (Vn.) 2
Viola (Va.)
Violoncello (Vc.)
Contrabass (Cb.)

I

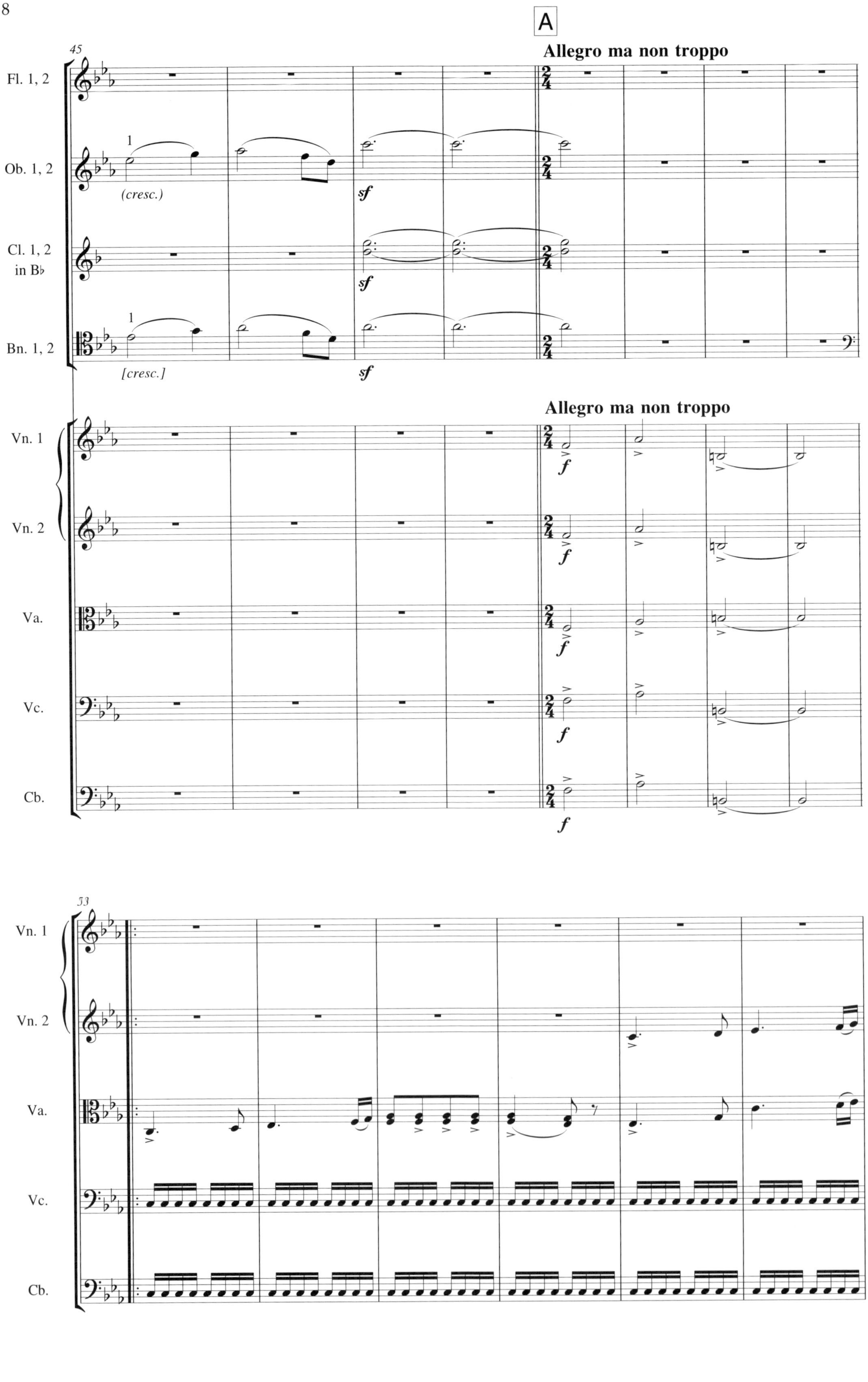
A
Allegro ma non troppo
45
Fl. 1, 2
Ob. 1, 2
(cresc.)
sf
Cl. 1, 2
in B♭
Bn. 1, 2
[cresc.]
Allegro ma non troppo
Vn. 1
Vn. 2
Va.
Vc.
Cb.
f
53

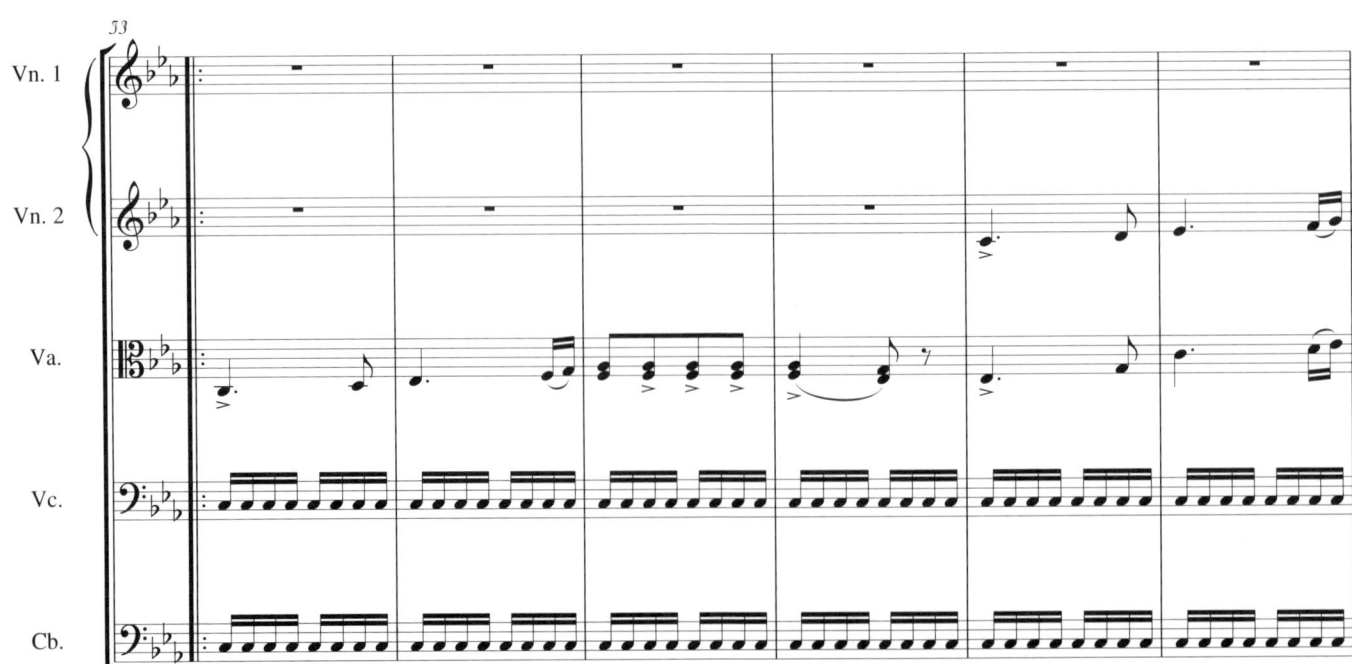

14

17

*See Editorial Methods, p. 346, col. 2.

155
Fl. 1, 2
Ob. 1, 2
Cl. 1, 2 in B♭
Bn. 1, 2
Hn. 1, 2 in E♭
Tpt. 1, 2 in C
A. Trb.
T. Trb.
B. Trb.
Timp.
Vn. 1
Vn. 2
Va.
Vc.
Cb.

163
Fl. 1, 2
Ob. 1, 2
Cl. 1, 2 in B♭
Bn. 1, 2
Hn. 1, 2 in E♭
Tpt. 1, 2 in C
A. Trb.
T. Trb.
B. Trb.
Timp.
Vn. 1
Vn. 2
Va.
Vc.
Cb.
cresc.
f

D
170
Fl. 1, 2
Ob. 1, 2
Cl. 1, 2
in B♭
molto dim.
Bn. 1, 2
molto dim.
1
p
Hn. 1, 2
in E♭
molto dim.
p
Tpt. 1, 2
in C
A. Trb.
T. Trb.
B. Trb.
Timp.
Vn. 1
Vn. 2
Va.
[molto dim.]
Vc.
[molto dim.]
Cb.
[molto dim.]

176
Cl. 1, 2 in B♭
Bn. 1, 2
Hn. 1, 2 in E♭
Vn. 1
Vn. 2
Va.
Vc.
184
Cl. 1, 2 in B♭
Bn. 1, 2
Hn. 1, 2 in E♭
Vn. 1
Vn. 2
Va.
Vc.
Cb.

23

201
Fl. 1, 2
Ob. 1, 2
Cl. 1, 2 in B♭
(cresc.)
Bn. 1, 2
Hn. 1, 2 in E♭
[cresc.]
Tpt. 1, 2 in C
A. Trb. T. Trb.
B. Trb.
Timp.
Vn. 1
Vn. 2
Va.
Vc.
Cb.

25

216
Fl. 1, 2
pp
Ob. 1, 2
Cl. 1, 2
in B♭
pp
Bn. 1, 2
Hn. 1, 2
in E♭
(pp)
Tpt. 1, 2
in C
A. Trb.
T. Trb.
B. Trb.
Timp.
Vn. 1
Vn. 2
Va.
p
Vc.
p
Cb.
p

222
Fl. 1, 2
Ob. 1, 2
Cl. 1, 2
in B♭
Bn. 1, 2
Hn. 1, 2
in E♭
Tpt. 1, 2
in C
A. Trb.
T. Trb.
B. Trb.
Timp.
Vn. 1
Vn. 2
Va.
Vc.
Cb.
1.
p
f

E
2.
231
Fl. 1, 2
Ob. 1, 2
Cl. 1, 2
in B♭
Bn. 1, 2
Hn. 1, 2
in E♭
Tpt. 1, 2
in C
A. Trb.
T. Trb.
B. Trb.
Timp.
Vn. 1
Vn. 2
Va.
Vc.
Cb.

239
Fl. 1, 2
mf
Ob. 1, 2
[cresc.]
mf
Cl. 1, 2
in B♭
[cresc.]
mf
Bn. 1, 2
[cresc.]
Hn. 1, 2
in E♭
[cresc.]
Tpt. 1, 2
in C
A. Trb.
T. Trb.
B. Trb.
Timp.
Vn. 1
mf cresc.
Vn. 2
cresc.
Va.
cresc.
Vc.
[cresc.]
Cb.
[cresc.]

247
Fl. 1, 2
p 3
Ob. 1, 2
p 3
(p)
Cl. 1, 2
in B♭
p
Bn. 1, 2
p 3
Hn. 1, 2
in E♭
Tpt. 1, 2
in C
A. Trb.
T. Trb.
B. Trb.
Timp.
Vn. 1
p
Vn. 2
p
Va.
p
Vc.
p
Cb.
p

31

258
Fl. 1, 2
Ob. 1, 2
Cl. 1, 2
in B♭
Bn. 1, 2
Hn. 1, 2
in E♭
Tpt. 1, 2
in C
A. Trb.
T. Trb.
B. Trb.
Timp.
Vn. 1
Vn. 2
Va.
Vc.
Cb.

F
263
Fl. 1, 2
Ob. 1, 2
Cl. 1, 2
in B♭
Bn. 1, 2
Hn. 1, 2
in E♭
Tpt. 1, 2
in C
A. Trb.
T. Trb.
B. Trb.
Timp.
Vn. 1
Vn. 2
Va.
Vc.
Cb.
f

34

275
Fl. 1, 2
Ob. 1, 2
1
p
Cl. 1, 2
in B♭
Bn. 1, 2
Hn. 1, 2
in E♭
Tpt. 1, 2
in C
A. Trb.
T. Trb.
B. Trb.
Timp.
Vn. 1
p
Vn. 2
Va.
Vc.
Cb.

280
Fl. 1, 2
Ob. 1, 2
Cl. 1, 2 in B♭
Bn. 1, 2
Hn. 1, 2 in E♭
Tpt. 1, 2 in C
A. Trb.
T. Trb.
B. Trb.
Timp.
Vn. 1
Vn. 2
Va.
Vc.
Cb.
[cresc.]
(cresc.)
p [cresc.]

285
Ob. 1, 2
Vn. 1
sempre ff
Vn. 2
sempre ff
Va.
sempre ff
Vc.
3
3
sempre ff
Cb.
3
3
291
a 2
Fl. 1, 2
f
a 2
Ob. 1, 2
f
a 2
Cl. 1, 2
in B♭
f
a 2
Bn. 1, 2
f
Vn. 1
ff
Vn. 2
Va.
(ff)
Vc.
Cb.
sempre ff

299
Fl. 1, 2
Ob. 1, 2
1 [solo]
Cl. 1, 2
in B♭
Bn. 1, 2
Hn. 1, 2
in E♭
Tpt. 1, 2
in C
A. Trb.
T. Trb.
(f)
B. Trb.
Timp.
Vn. 1
Vn. 2
Va.
Vc.
Cb.

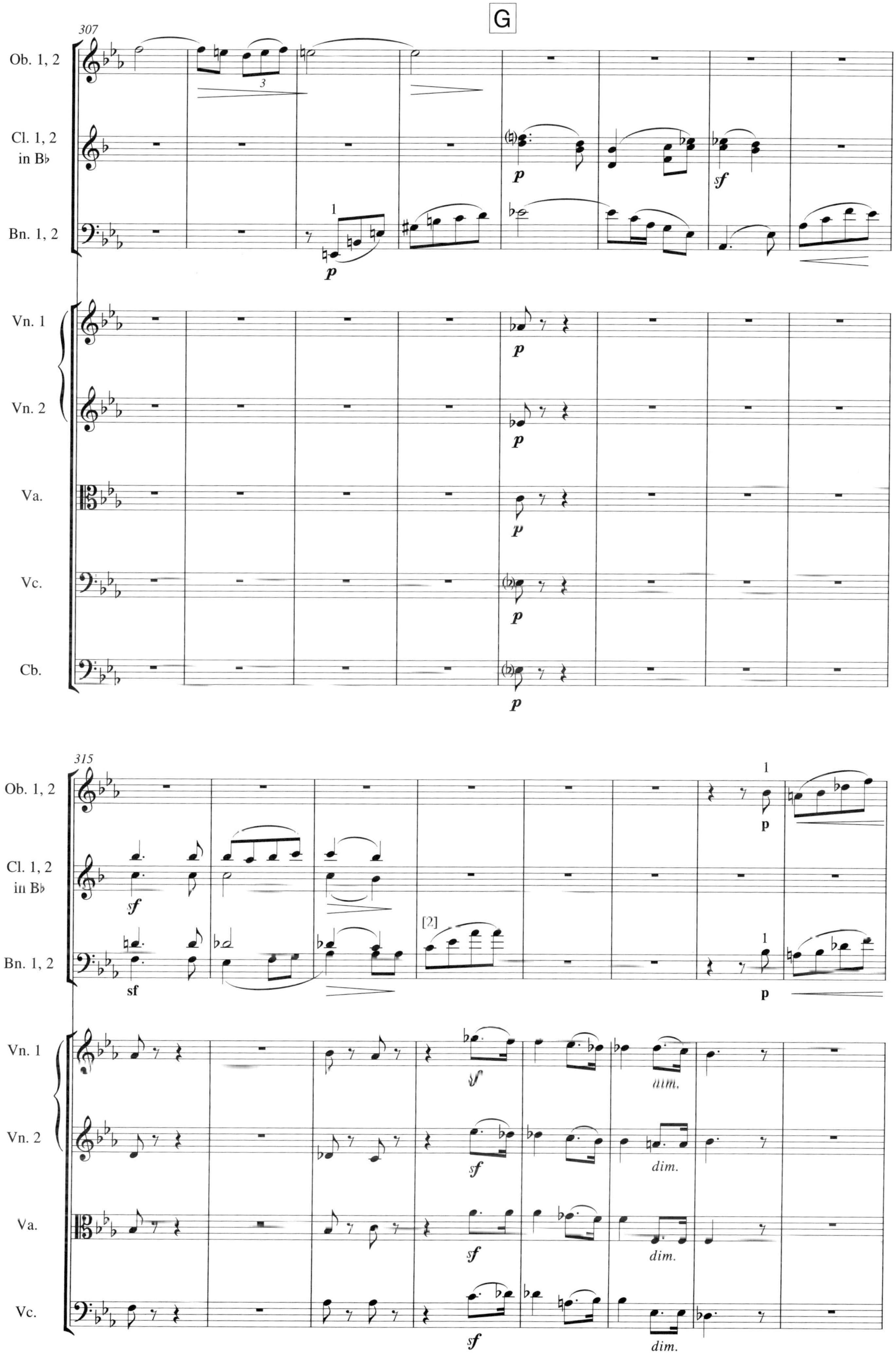
G
307
Ob. 1, 2
Cl. 1, 2 in B♭
Bn. 1, 2
Vn. 1
Vn. 2
Va.
Vc.
Cb.
p
sf
315
[2]
dim.

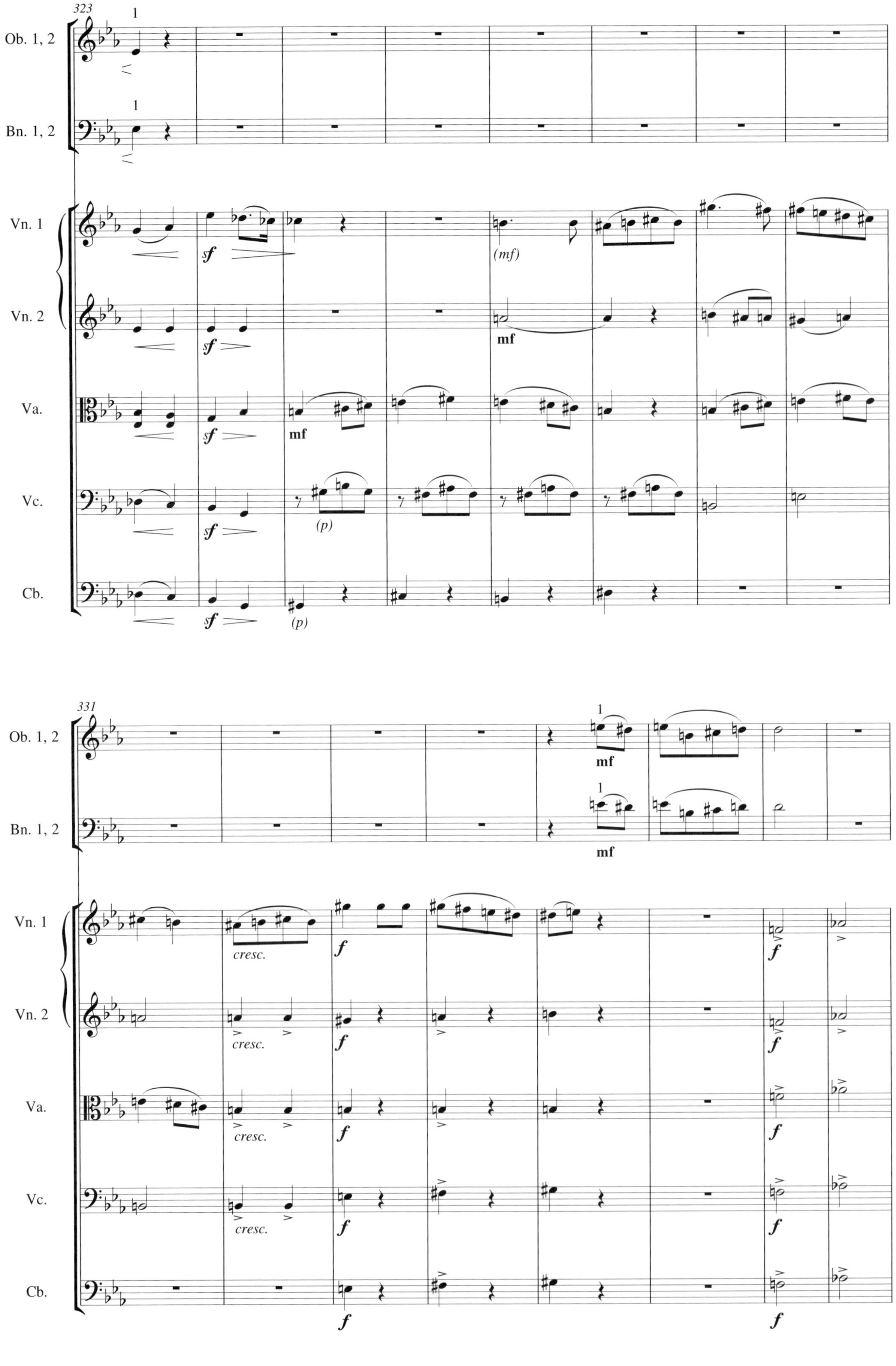
323
Ob. 1, 2
Bn. 1, 2
Vn. 1
Vn. 2
Va.
Vc.
Cb.
sf
(mf)
mf
(p)
331
cresc.
f

339
Fl. 1, 2
Ob. 1, 2
cresc.
Cl. 1, 2
in B♭
Bn. 1, 2
cresc.
Hn. 1, 2
in E♭
Tpt. 1, 2
in C
A. Trb.
T. Trb.
B. Trb.
Timp.
Vn. 1
f
Vn. 2
f
Va.
Vc.
Cb.

348
Fl. 1, 2
Ob. 1, 2
Cl. 1, 2
in B♭
Bn. 1, 2
Hn. 1, 2
in E♭
Tpt. 1, 2
in C
A. Trb.
T. Trb.
B. Trb.
Timp.
Vn. 1
Vn. 2
Va.
Vc.
Cb.

356
Cl. 1, 2
in B♭
Bn. 1, 2
B. Trb.
[solo]
(p)
sf
Vn. 1
ff
dim.
p
Vn. 2
ff
dim.
p
Va.
ff
dim.
p
Vc.
ff
p
sf
p
362
Cl. 1, 2
in B♭
pp
Bn. 1, 2
pp
Vn. 1
p
(sempre p)
Vn. 2
p
Va.
Vc.

368
Cl. 1, 2
in B♭
Bn. 1, 2
Hn. 1, 2
in E♭
1
p
Vn. 1
sf
Vn. 2
(pp)
sfp
Va.
(pp)
sfp
Vc.
pp
sfp
374
Cl. 1, 2
in B♭
p
dim.
Bn. 1, 2
p
dim.
Vn. 1
Vn. 2
Va.
Vc.
pp
Cb.
pp

380
Fl. 1, 2
pp
Ob. 1, 2
Cl. 1, 2
in B♭
pp
Bn. 1, 2
1
pp
a 2
(p)
Hn. 1, 2
in E♭
1
pp
a 2
(p)
Tpt. 1, 2
in C
A. Trb.
T. Trb.
B. Trb.
Timp.
tr
pp
Vn. 1
pp
(pp)
Vn. 2
pp
(pp)
Va.
pp
(pp)
Vc.
pp
(pp)
Cb.
pp
(pp)

387
Fl. 1, 2
Ob. 1, 2
pp
Cl. 1, 2
in B♭
Bn. 1, 2
Hn. 1, 2
in E♭
Tpt. 1, 2
in C
A. Trb.
T. Trb.
B. Trb.
(tr)
Timp.
Vn. 1
pp
sempre pp
Vn. 2
pp
sempre pp
Va.
pp
sempre pp
Vc.
sempre pp
Cb.
sempre pp

47

405
Fl. 1, 2
Ob. 1, 2
Cl. 1, 2
in B♭
Bn. 1, 2
Hn. 1, 2
in E♭
Tpt. 1, 2
in C
A. Trb.
T. Trb.
B. Trb.
Timp.
Vn. 1
Vn. 2
Va.
Vc.
Cb.

49

421
Fl. 1, 2
Ob. 1, 2
Cl. 1, 2
in B♭
Bn. 1, 2
Hn. 1, 2
in E♭
Tpt. 1, 2
in C
A. Trb.
T. Trb.
B. Trb.
Timp.
Vn. 1
Vn. 2
Va.
Vc.
Cb.

426
Fl. 1, 2
a 2
Ob. 1, 2
1
a 2
Cl. 1, 2
in B♭
Bn. 1, 2
a 2
Hn. 1, 2
in E♭
[muta in C]
Tpt. 1, 2
in C
A. Trb.
T. Trb.
B. Trb.
Timp.
tr
mf
(f)
Vn. 1
Vn. 2
Va.
Vc.
Cb.

432
Fl. 1, 2
Ob. 1, 2
Cl. 1, 2 in B♭
Bn. 1, 2
Hn. 1, 2 in C
Tpt. 1, 2 in C
A. Trb.
T. Trb.
B. Trb.
Timp.
Vn. 1
Vn. 2
Va.
Vc.
Cb.
sempre f

438
Fl. 1, 2
[solo]
Ob. 1, 2
p
sf
Cl. 1, 2
in B♭
Bn. 1, 2
Hn. 1, 2
in C
Corni in C
1
(p)
Tpt. 1, 2
in C
A. Trb.
T. Trb.
B. Trb.
Timp.
Vn. 1
Vn. 2
Va.
Vc.
Cb.

447
I
Vn. 1
Vn. 2
Va.
Vc.
Cb.
p
456
Fl. 1, 2
Ob. 1, 2
Cl. 1, 2
in B♭
Bn. 1, 2
Vn. 1
Vn. 2
Va.
Vc.
Cb.
1
p
(p)

465
Fl. 1, 2
Ob. 1, 2
Cl. 1, 2
in B♭
Bn. 1, 2
Hn. 1, 2
in C
Tpt. 1, 2
in C
A. Trb.
T. Trb.
B. Trb.
Timp.
Vn. 1
Vn. 2
Va.
Vc.
Cb.

473
Fl. 1, 2
Ob. 1, 2
Cl. 1, 2
in B♭
Bn. 1, 2
Hn. 1, 2
in C
Tpt. 1, 2
in C
A. Trb.
T. Trb.
B. Trb.
Timp.
Vn. 1
Vn. 2
Va.
Vc.
Cb.
cresc.
f

L
480
Fl. 1, 2
[1]
Ob. 1, 2
[dim.]
Cl. 1, 2
in B♭
[dim.]
Bn. 1, 2
[dim.]
Hn. 1, 2
in C
p
Tpt. 1, 2
in C
A. Trb.
T. Trb.
B. Trb.
Timp.
Vn. 1
dim.
Vn. 2
dim.
Va.
dim.
Vc.
dim.
p
Cb.
dim.

487
Cl. 1, 2
in B♭
Bn. 1, 2
Hn. 1, 2
in C
Vn. 1
Vn. 2
Va.
Vc.
sf
p
1
dim.
495
Cl. 1, 2
in B♭
Bn. 1, 2
Hn. 1, 2
in C
Vn. 1
Vn. 2
Va.
Vc.
Cb.
(p)

59

511
Fl. 1, 2
Ob. 1, 2
Cl. 1, 2
in B♭
Bn. 1, 2
Hn. 1, 2
in C
Tpt. 1, 2
in C
A. Trb.
T. Trb.
B. Trb.
Timp.
Vn. 1
Vn. 2
Va.
Vc.
Cb.
[cresc.]
[cresc.]
p
cresc.
cresc.
cresc.
cresc.
cresc.

517
Fl. 1, 2
f
p dim.
Ob. 1, 2
f
p dim.
1
Cl. 1, 2
in B♭
f
p dim.
Bn. 1, 2
1
f
p
Hn. 1, 2
in C
[cresc.]
f
p
Tpt. 1, 2
in C
A. Trb.
T. Trb.
B. Trb.
Timp.
Vn. 1
f
Vn. 2
f
Va.
3
f
Vc.
f
p
Cb.
f
p

525
Fl. 1, 2
Ob. 1, 2
Cl. 1, 2
in B♭
1
[cresc.]
Bn. 1, 2
[cresc.]
Hn. 1, 2
in C
(cresc.)
Tpt. 1, 2
in C
A. Trb.
T. Trb.
B. Trb.
Timp.
Vn. 1
p
cresc.
Vn. 2
p
cresc.
Va.
p
cresc.
Vc.
cresc.
Cb.
cresc.

63

M
540
Fl. 1, 2
Ob. 1, 2
Cl. 1, 2
in B♭
Bn. 1, 2
Hn. 1, 2
in C
Tpt. 1, 2
in C
A. Trb.
T. Trb.
B. Trb.
Timp.
Vn. 1
Vn. 2
Va.
Vc.
Cb.
pp
(pp)
tr
mf

65

558
Fl. 1, 2
[cresc.]
Ob. 1, 2
[cresc.]
Cl. 1, 2 in B♭
[cresc.]
Bn. 1, 2
[cresc.]
Hn. 1, 2 in C
Tpt. 1, 2 in C
A. Trb.
T. Trb.
B. Trb.
Timp.
Vn. 1
Vn. 2
Va.
Vc.
Cb.

67

568
accel.
Fl. 1, 2
Ob. 1, 2
Cl. 1, 2 in B♭
Bn. 1, 2
Hn. 1, 2 in C
Tpt. 1, 2 in C
A. Trb.
T. Trb.
B. Trb.
Timp.
accel.
Vn. 1
Vn. 2
Va.
Vc.
Cb.

573
Fl. 1, 2
Ob. 1, 2
Cl. 1, 2
in B♭
Bn. 1, 2
Hn. 1, 2
in C
Tpt. 1, 2
in C
A. Trb.
T. Trb.
B. Trb.
Timp.
Vn. 1
Vn. 2
Va.
Vc.
Cb.
a 2
ff
tr

578
a 2
Fl. 1, 2
Ob. 1, 2
Cl. 1, 2
in B♭
Bn. 1, 2
Hn. 1, 2
in C
Tpt. 1, 2
in C
A. Trb.
T. Trb.
B. Trb.
(tr)
Timp.
Vn. 1
Vn. 2
Va.
Vc.
Cb.

584
Fl. 1, 2
Ob. 1, 2
Cl. 1, 2
in B♭
Bn. 1, 2
Hn. 1, 2
in C
Tpt. 1, 2
in C
A. Trb.
T. Trb.
B. Trb.
Timp.
Vn. 1
Vn. 2
Va.
Vc.
Cb.
ff
f

II

7
Fl. 1, 2
Bn. 1, 2
Hn. 1, 2
in A♭
Vn. 1
Vn. 2
Va.
Vc.
(p)
pp
p
14
dim.
(dim.)
[dim.]
cresc.
(cresc.)
[cresc.]

A
21
Cl. 1, 2 in B♭
1
pp
[solo]
p
Hn. 1, 2 in A♭
Vn. 1
pp
Vn. 2
(pp)
Va.
(pp)
Vc.
pp
Cb.
27
Cl. 1, 2 in B♭
Hn. 1, 2 in A♭
(cresc.)
Vn. 1
[cresc.]
Vn. 2
[cresc.]
Va.
[cresc.]
Vc.
Cb.

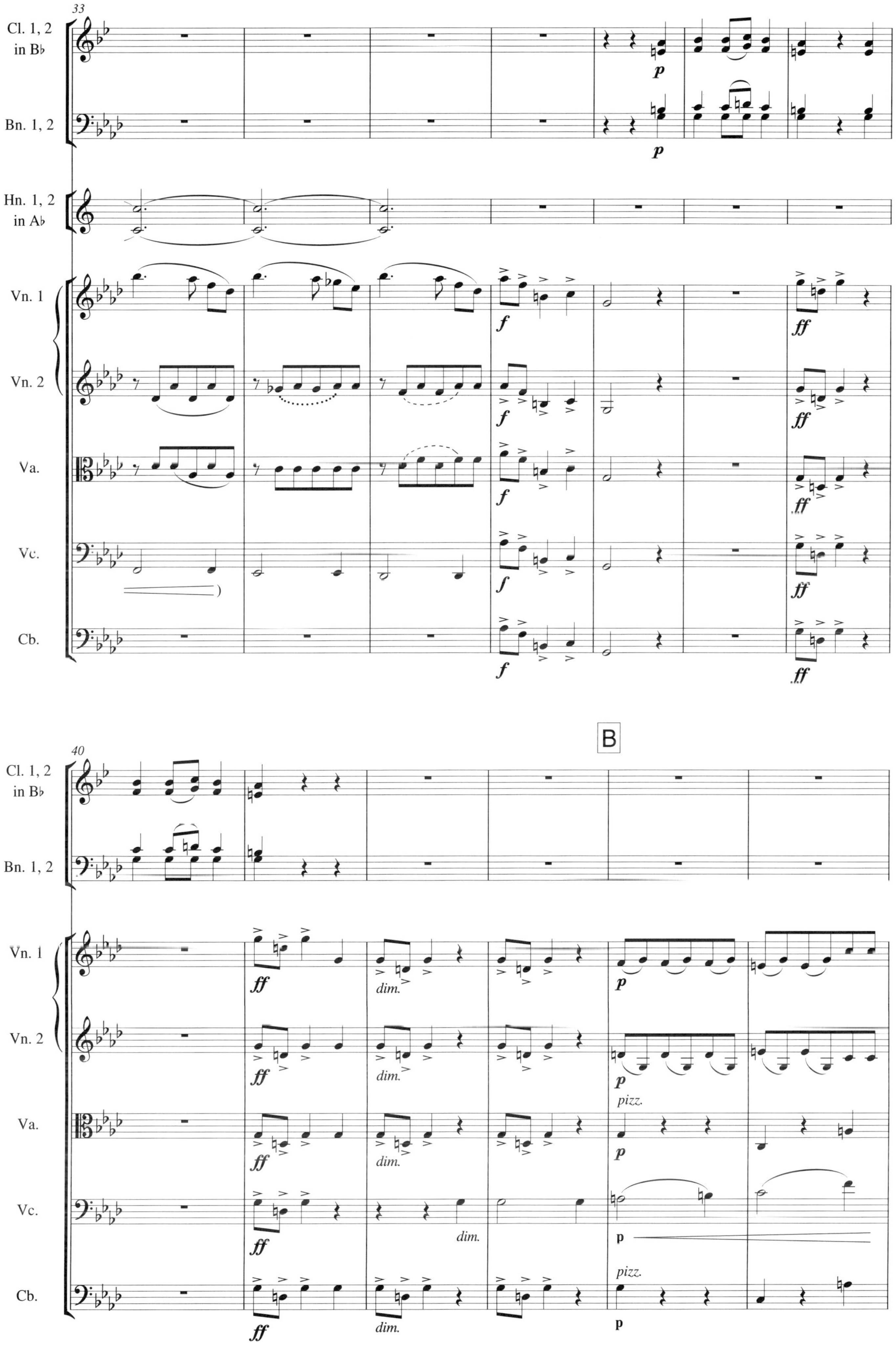
33
Cl. 1, 2
in B♭
Bn. 1, 2
Hn. 1, 2
in A♭
Vn. 1
Vn. 2
Va.
Vc.
Cb.
p
f
ff
40
B
dim.
pizz.

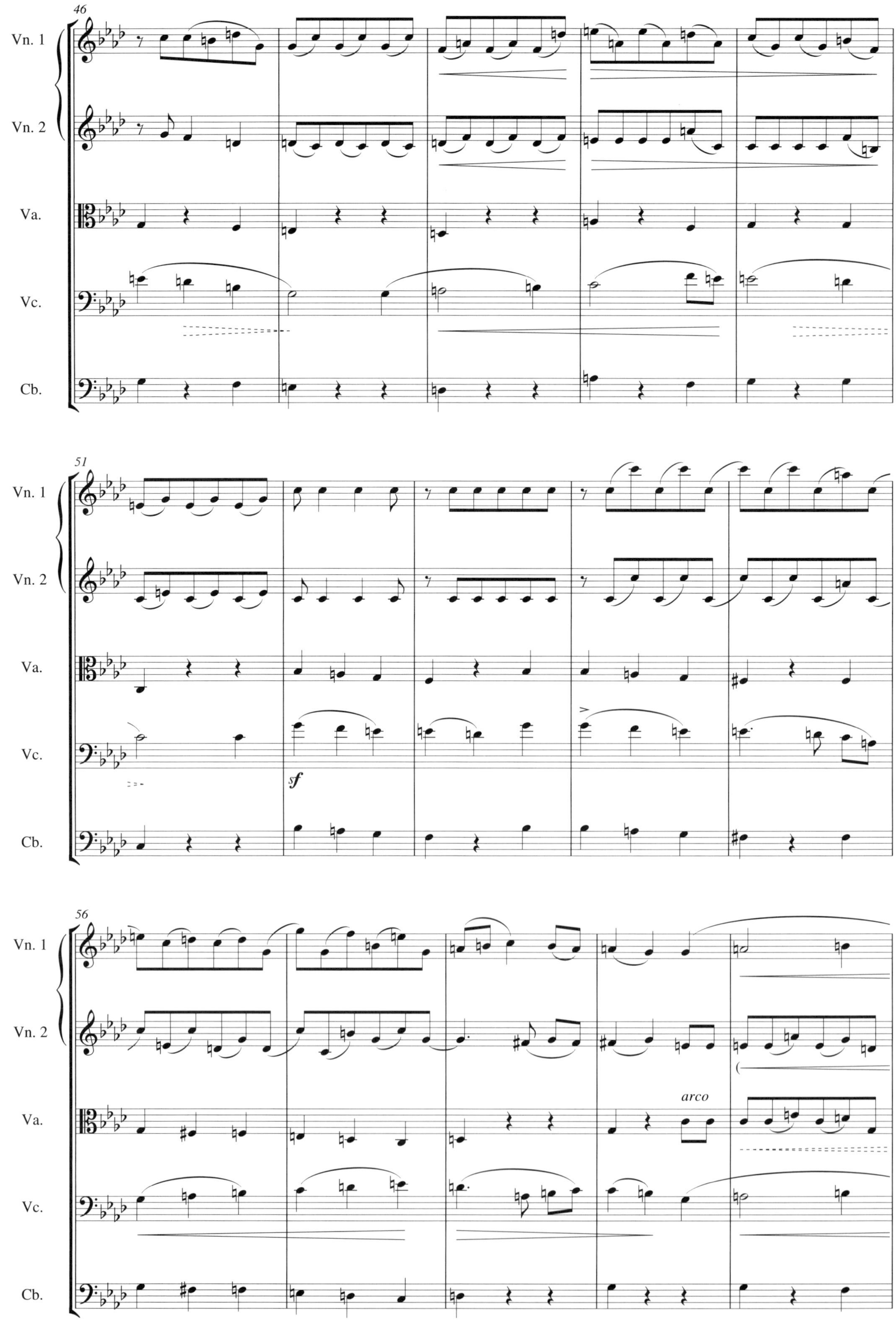
46
Vn. 1
Vn. 2
Va.
Vc.
Cb.
51
Vn. 1
Vn. 2
Va.
Vc.
sf
Cb.
56
Vn. 1
Vn. 2
Va.
arco
Vc.
Cb.

77

73
1
Cl. 1, 2
in B♭
Vn. 1
Vn. 2
Va.
Vc.
pizz.
arco
Cb.
pizz.
78
Cl. 1, 2
in B♭
Bn. 1, 2
Hn. 1, 2
in A♭
Vn. 1
cresc.
Vn. 2
cresc.
Va.
cresc.
Vc.
arco
cresc.
Cb.
arco
cresc.

83
Fl. 1, 2
Ob. 1, 2
Cl. 1, 2
in B♭
sf
Bn. 1, 2
1
sf
Hn. 1, 2
in A♭
1
sf
Vn. 1
sf
Vn. 2
sf
Va.
sf
Vc.
Cb.

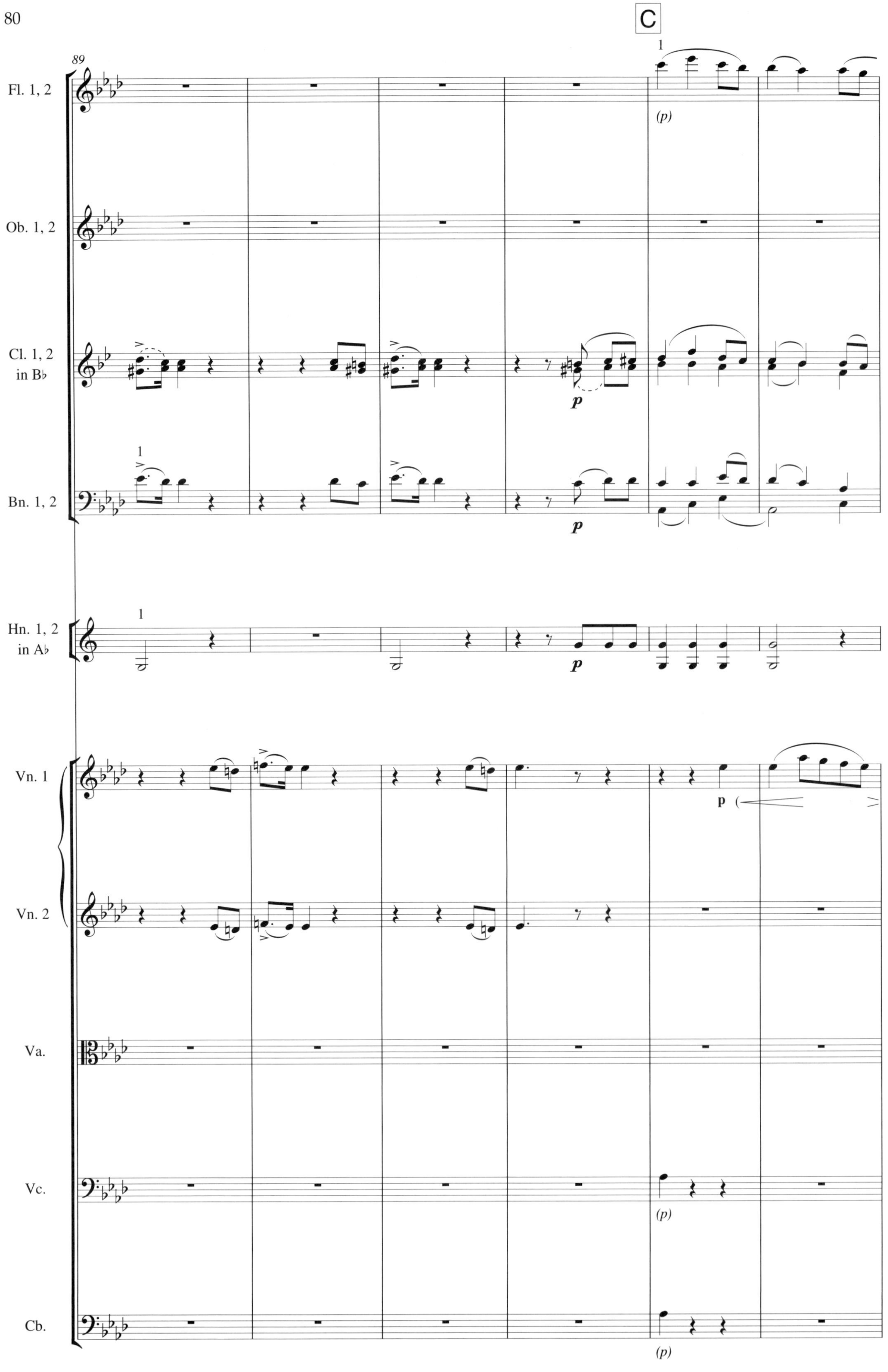
C
89
Fl. 1, 2
Ob. 1, 2
Cl. 1, 2
in B♭
Bn. 1, 2
Hn. 1, 2
in A♭
Vn. 1
Vn. 2
Va.
Vc.
Cb.
(p)
p

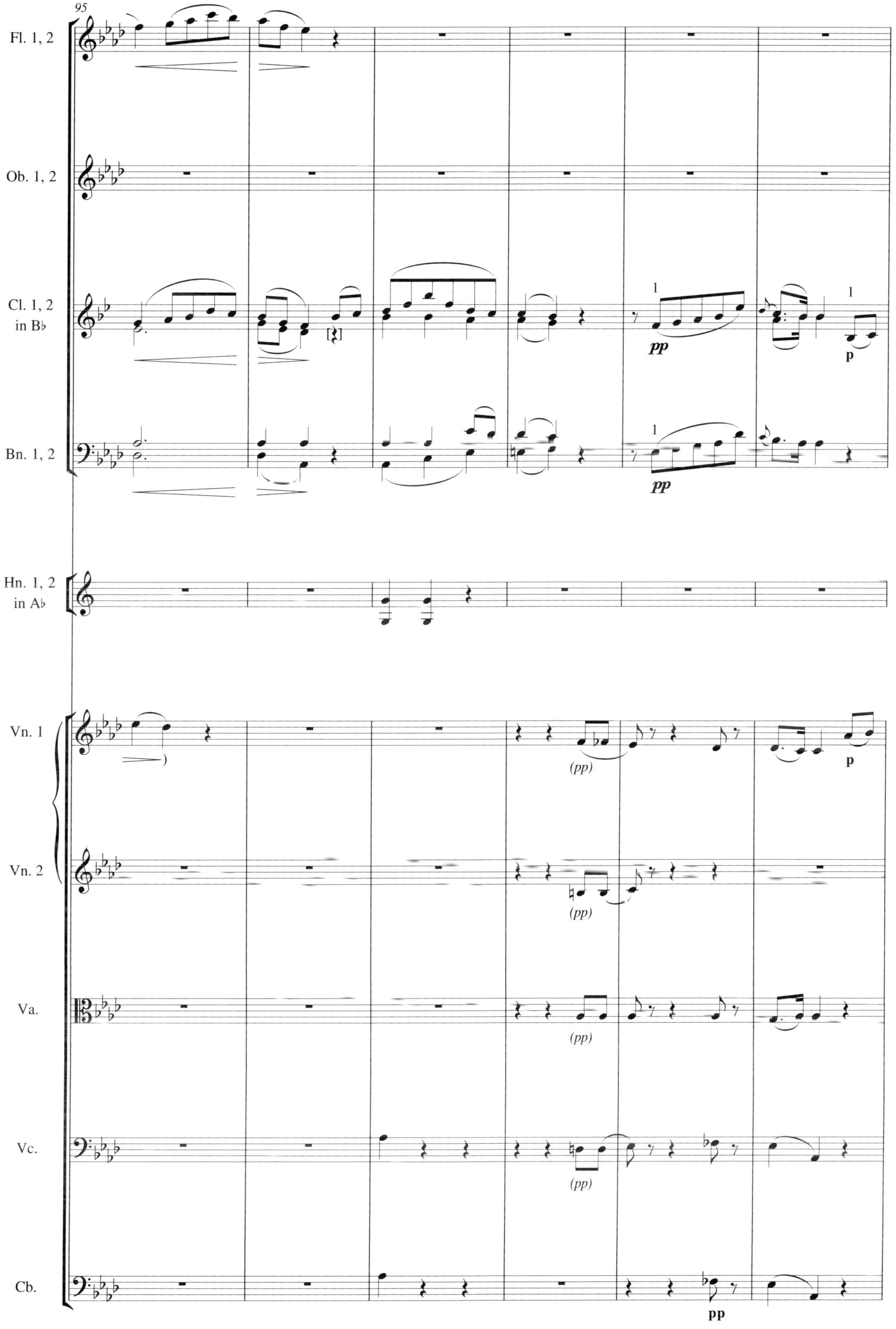
95
Fl. 1, 2
Ob. 1, 2
Cl. 1, 2
in B♭
Bn. 1, 2
Hn. 1, 2
in A♭
Vn. 1
Vn. 2
Va.
Vc.
Cb.
pp
p
(pp)
pp

101
Fl. 1, 2
Cl. 1, 2
in B♭
Bn. 1, 2
Vn. 1
Vn. 2
Va.
Vc.
p
(p)
107
Fl. 1, 2
Cl. 1, 2
in B♭
Bn. 1, 2
Vn. 1
Vn. 2
Va.
Vc.
Cb.
dim.
[più] f
(cresc.)
(dim.)
[dim.]
(più f)

83

125
Cl. 1, 2 in B♭
p
Bn. 1, 2
1
p
Hn. 1, 2 in A♭
1
p
Vn. 1
ff
(dim.)
Vn. 2
ff
(dim.)
Va.
ff
(dim.)
Vc.
ff
(dim.)
Cb.
ff
(dim.)
132
D
Fl. 1, 2
1
tr
pp
Vn. 1
p
Vn. 2
3
p
Va.
p
Vc.
p
Cb.

85

144
Fl. 1, 2
sf
Ob. 1, 2
sf
1
p
Cl. 1, 2
in B♭
1
[cresc.]
[cresc.]
Bn. 1, 2
sf
Hn. 1, 2
in A♭
Vn. 1
(cresc.)
sf
Vn. 2
(cresc.)
sf
Va.
(cresc.)
(cresc.)
Vc.
[cresc.]
sf
Cb.
[cresc.]
sf

150
Ob. 1, 2
dim.
Cl. 1, 2
in B♭
sf
p
Bn. 1, 2
1
sf
p
Hn. 1, 2
in A♭
sf
p
Vc.
(pp)
Cb.
(pp)
156
Cl. 1, 2
in B♭
1
pp
Bn. 1, 2
1
(pp)
Hn. 1, 2
in A♭
Vn. 1
(pp)
Vn. 2
(pp)
Va.
(pp)
Vc.
(pp)
Cb.

162
Fl. 1, 2
Ob. 1, 2
Cl. 1, 2 in B♭
Bn. 1, 2
Hn. 1, 2 in A♭
Vn. 1
Vn. 2
Va.
Vc.
Cb.
rall.
f
pp
morendo
cresc.
rall.
morendo
cresc.
morendo
cresc.
morendo
cresc.
morendo
cresc.
morendo

III

9
Fl. 1, 2
Ob. 1, 2
Cl. 1, 2 in B♭
Bn. 1, 2
Hn. 1, 2 in E♭
Tpt. 1, 2 in C
A. Trb.
T. Trb.
B. Trb.
Timp.
Vn. 1
Vn. 2
Va.
Vc.
Cb.
p
[>]

19
Fl. 1, 2
Ob. 1, 2
a 2
Cl. 1, 2
in B♭
Bn. 1, 2
a 2
Hn. 1, 2
in E♭
Tpt. 1, 2
in C
A. Trb.
T. Trb.
B. Trb.
Timp.
Vn. 1
p
Vn. 2
p
Va.
p
Vc.
p
Cb.
p

28
Fl. 1, 2
Ob. 1, 2
a 2
Cl. 1, 2
in B♭
Bn. 1, 2
a 2
Hn. 1, 2
in E♭
Tpt. 1, 2
in C
A. Trb.
T. Trb.
B. Trb.
Timp.
Vn. 1
f
Vn. 2
f
Va.
f
Vc.
Cb.

37
Fl. 1, 2
Ob. 1, 2
Cl. 1, 2
in B♭
Bn. 1, 2
Hn. 1, 2
in E♭
Tpt. 1, 2
in C
A. Trb.
T. Trb.
B. Trb.
Timp.
Vn. 1
Vn. 2
Va.
Vc.
Cb.
p

A
46
Fl. 1, 2
Ob. 1, 2
a 2
Cl. 1, 2
in B♭
p
Bn. 1, 2
p
Hn. 1, 2
in E♭
Tpt. 1, 2
in C
1
p
A. Trb.
T. Trb.
B. Trb.
Timp.
Vn. 1
Vn. 2
Va.
Vc.
Cb.

54
Fl. 1, 2
Ob. 1, 2
Cl. 1, 2
in B♭
a 2
Bn. 1, 2
Hn. 1, 2
in E♭
Tpt. 1, 2
in C
A. Trb.
T. Trb.
B. Trb.
Timp.
Vn. 1
p
Vn. 2
p
Va.
p
Vc.
p
Cb.
p

62
Poco meno mosso
Fl. 1, 2
Ob. 1, 2
a 2
1 [solo]
Cl. 1, 2
in B♭
Bn. 1, 2
Hn. 1, 2
in E♭
Tpt. 1, 2
in C
1
A. Trb.
T. Trb.
B. Trb.
Timp.
Poco meno mosso
Vn. 1
sfp
sf
Vn. 2
p
Va.
p
Vc.
p
Cb.

72
Fl. 1, 2
Ob. 1, 2
Cl. 1, 2
in B♭
Bn. 1, 2
Hn. 1, 2
in E♭
Tpt. 1, 2
in C
A. Trb.
T. Trb.
B. Trb.
Timp.
Vn. 1
Vn. 2
Va.
Vc.
Cb.

81
Fl. 1, 2
Ob. 1, 2
Cl. 1, 2
in B♭
Bn. 1, 2
Hn. 1, 2
in E♭
Tpt. 1, 2
in C
A. Trb.
T. Trb.
B. Trb.
Timp.
Vn. 1
Vn. 2
Va.
Vc.
Cb.
1
p
cresc.
[cresc.]

90
Fl. 1, 2
Ob. 1, 2
Cl. 1, 2
in B♭
Bn. 1, 2
Vn. 1
Vn. 2
Va.
Vc.
pp
(pp)
p
dim.
(p)
98
Fl. 1, 2
Ob. 1, 2
Cl. 1, 2
in B♭
Vn. 1
Vn. 2
Va.
Vc.
p

B
Tempo I
104
Fl. 1, 2
Ob. 1, 2
Cl. 1, 2
in B♭
Bn. 1, 2
Hn. 1, 2
in E♭
Tpt. 1, 2
in C
A. Trb.
T. Trb.
B. Trb.
Timp.
Vn. 1
Vn. 2
Va.
Vc.
Cb.
dim.
p
sf

C
113
Fl. 1, 2
cresc.
ff
Ob. 1, 2
[cresc.]
ff
Cl. 1, 2
in B♭
cresc.
ff
Bn. 1, 2
cresc.
ff
Hn. 1, 2
in E♭
cresc.
ff
Tpt. 1, 2
in C
a 2
(ff)
A. Trb.
T. Trb.
(ff)
B. Trb.
(ff)
Timp.
tr
(ff)
Vn. 1
ff
Vn. 2
ff
Va.
ff
Vc.
ff
Cb.
ff

122
Fl. 1, 2
Ob. 1, 2
Cl. 1, 2
in B♭
Bn. 1, 2
Hn. 1, 2
in E♭
Tpt. 1, 2
in C
a 2
A. Trb.
T. Trb.
B. Trb.
Timp.
Vn. 1
Vn. 2
Va.
Vc.
Cb.

132
Vn. 1
Vn. 2
Va.
Vc.
Cb.
cresc.
cresc.
cresc.
cresc.
cresc.
140
Fl. 1, 2
Ob. 1, 2
Cl. 1, 2 in B♭
Timp.
Vn. 1
Vn. 2
Va.
Vc.
Cb.
ff
f [cresc.]
f [cresc.]
(f) [cresc.]
cresc.
cresc.

148
Fl. 1, 2
Ob. 1, 2
Cl. 1, 2
in B♭
Bn. 1, 2
Hn. 1, 2
in E♭
Tpt. 1, 2
in C
A. Trb.
T. Trb.
B. Trb.
Timp.
Vn. 1
Vn. 2
Va.
Vc.
Cb.
ff
p
mf

105

D
164
Cl. 1, 2
in B♭
(mf)
Bn. 1, 2
mf
A. Trb.
T. Trb.
p
B. Trb.
p
Vn. 1
f
Vn. 2
f
Va.
f
Vc.
f
Cb.
f
173
Vn. 1
Vn. 2
Va.
Vc.
Cb.

181
Fl. 1, 2
Ob. 1, 2
Cl. 1, 2
in B♭
Bn. 1, 2
Vn. 1
Vn. 2
Va.
Vc.
Cb.
1
(sf)
sf
1 [solo]
dim.
Poco meno mosso
Poco meno mosso
190
Ob. 1, 2
Hn. 1, 2
in E♭
1 [solo]
p
Vn. 1
Vn. 2
Va.
Vc.

199
Fl. 1, 2
Ob. 1, 2
Cl. 1, 2 in B♭
Bn. 1, 2
Hn. 1, 2 in E♭
Tpt. 1, 2 in C
A. Trb.
T. Trb.
B. Trb.
Timp.
Vn. 1
Vn. 2
Va.
Vc.
Cb.
a 2
sf
(sf)
p
tr

208
Fl. 1, 2
1 solo
cresc.
Ob. 1, 2
1
pp
Cl. 1, 2
in B♭
1 solo
cresc.
1
p
Bn. 1, 2
pp
Hn. 1, 2
in E♭
a 2
1
pp
Tpt. 1, 2
in C
A. Trb.
T. Trb.
B. Trb.
Timp.
Vn. 1
(cresc.)
Vn. 2
[cresc.]
p
Va.
[cresc.]
(p)
Vc.
[cresc.]
pizz.
p
Cb.
[cresc.]

217
Fl. 1, 2
Ob. 1, 2
Cl. 1, 2
in B♭
Bn. 1, 2
Hn. 1, 2
in E♭
Tpt. 1, 2
in C
A. Trb.
T. Trb.
B. Trb.
Timp.
Vn. 1
Vn. 2
Va.
Vc.
Cb.

111

E
232
accel.
a 2
Fl. 1, 2
Ob. 1, 2
Cl. 1, 2
in B♭
Bn. 1, 2
Hn. 1, 2
in E♭
Tpt. 1, 2
in C
A. Trb.
T. Trb.
B. Trb.
Timp.
accel.
Vn. 1
Vn. 2
Va.
Vc.
Cb.

113

246
Fl. 1, 2
a 2
Ob. 1, 2
Cl. 1, 2
in B♭
a 2
Bn. 1, 2
Hn. 1, 2
in E♭
a 2
Tpt. 1, 2
in C
a 2
A. Trb.
T. Trb.
B. Trb.
Timp.
f
f
Vn. 1
Vn. 2
Va.
Vc.
Cb.

255
Fl. 1, 2
Ob. 1, 2
Cl. 1, 2
in B♭
Bn. 1, 2
Hn. 1, 2
in E♭
Tpt. 1, 2
in C
A. Trb.
T. Trb.
B. Trb.
Timp.
Vn. 1
Vn. 2
Va.
Vc.
Cb.
ff

accel.
263
Fl. 1, 2
Ob. 1, 2
a 2
Cl. 1, 2 in B♭
Bn. 1, 2
a 2
Hn. 1, 2 in E♭
Tpt. 1, 2 in C
a 2
A. Trb. T. Trb.
B. Trb.
Timp.
accel.
Vn. 1
Vn. 2
Va.
Vc.
Cb.

271
Fl. 1, 2
cresc.
Ob. 1, 2
cresc.
Cl. 1, 2 in B♭
cresc.
Bn. 1, 2
cresc.
Hn. 1, 2 in E♭
Tpt. 1, 2 in C
A. Trb.
T. Trb.
B. Trb.
Timp.
tr
(ff)
Vn. 1
cresc.
Vn. 2
cresc.
Va.
[cresc.]
Vc.
[cresc.]
Cb.
[cresc.]

280
a 2
Fl. 1, 2
Ob. 1, 2
a 2
Cl. 1, 2 in B♭
Bn. 1, 2
Hn. 1, 2 in E♭
a 2
Tpt. 1, 2 in C
A. Trb.
T. Trb.
B. Trb.
(tr)
Timp.
Vn. 1
Vn. 2
Va.
Vc.
Cb.

288
Fl. 1, 2
Ob. 1, 2
Cl. 1, 2
in B♭
Bn. 1, 2
Hn. 1, 2
in E♭
Tpt. 1, 2
in C
A. Trb.
T. Trb.
B. Trb.
Timp.
Vn. 1
Vn. 2
Va.
Vc.
Cb.

296
Fl. 1, 2
Ob. 1, 2
Cl. 1, 2
in B♭
Bn. 1, 2
Hn. 1, 2
in E♭
Tpt. 1, 2
in C
A. Trb.
T. Trb.
B. Trb.
Timp.
Vn. 1
Vn. 2
Va.
Vc.
Cb.
a 2
ff

IV

*See Critical Notes.

6
Fl. 1, 2
Ob. 1, 2
Cl. 1, 2
in B♭
Bn. 1, 2
a 2
3
Hn. 1, 2
in C
a 2
Tpt. 1, 2
in C
a 2
A. Trb.
T. Trb.
B. Trb.
Timp.
Vn. 1
Vn. 2
Va.
Vc.
3
Cb.
3

123

16
a 2
Fl. 1, 2
1
p
Ob. 1, 2
1
p
Cl. 1, 2
in B♭
Bn. 1, 2
a 2
Hn. 1, 2
in C
a 2
Tpt. 1, 2
in C
A. Trb.
T. Trb.
B. Trb.
Timp.
Vn. 1
dim.
sf
Vn. 2
(dim.)
(p)
sf
Va.
[dim.]
p
sf
Vc.
(p)
Cb.
(p)

21
a 2
A
Fl. 1, 2
ff
Ob. 1, 2
ff
Cl. 1, 2
in B♭
ff
Bn. 1, 2
ff
Hn. 1, 2
in C
a 2
ff
Tpt. 1, 2
in C
a 2
ff
A. Trb.
T. Trb.
ff
B. Trb.
ff
Timp.
f
Vn. 1
ff
p
Vn. 2
ff
(p)
Va.
ff
(p)
Vc.
ff
(p)
Cb.
ff
(p)

126

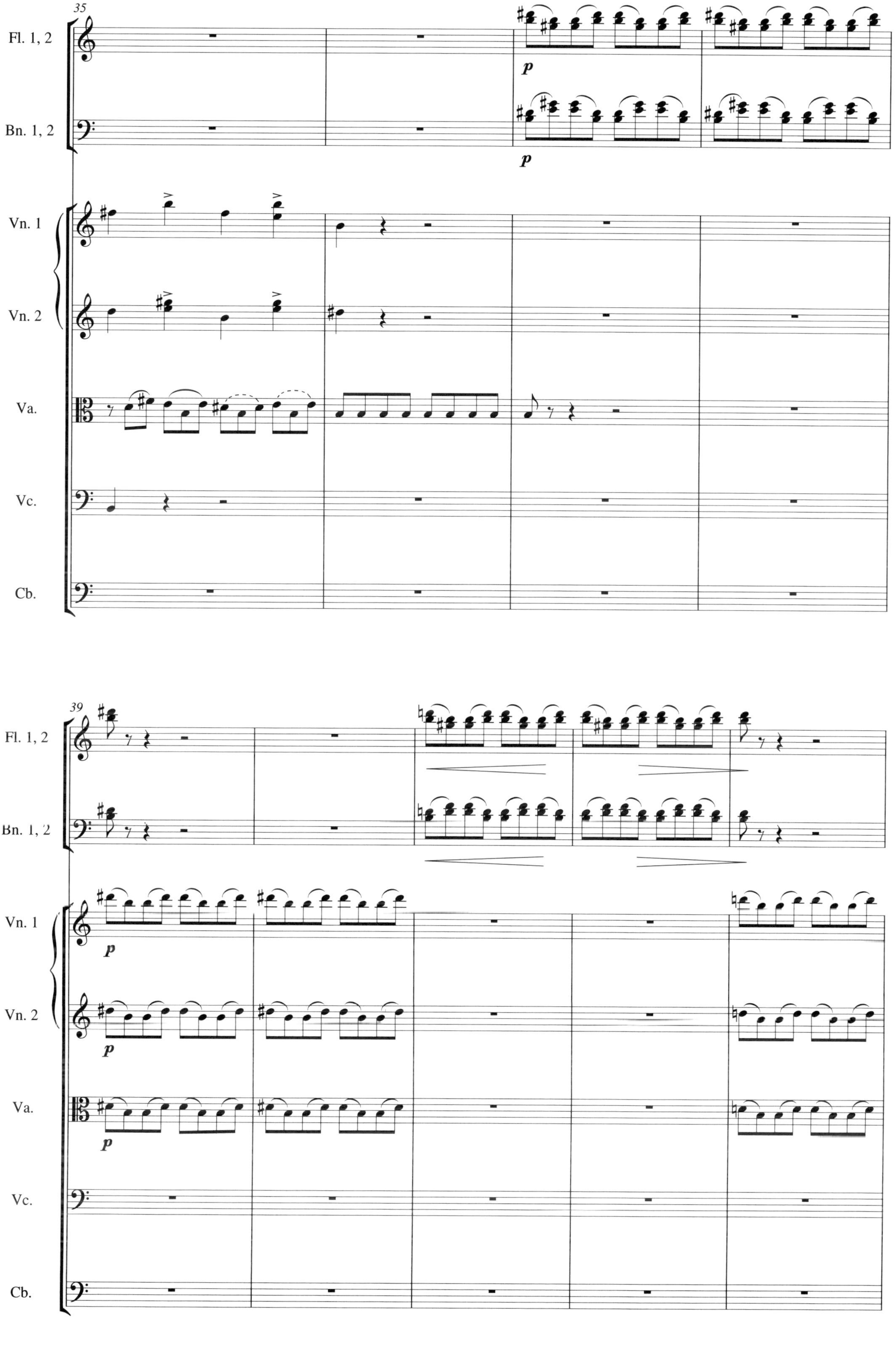
35
Fl. 1, 2
Bn. 1, 2
Vn. 1
Vn. 2
Va.
Vc.
Cb.
p
p
39
Fl. 1, 2
Bn. 1, 2
Vn. 1
Vn. 2
Va.
Vc.
Cb.
p
p
p

44
Fl. 1, 2
Hn. 1, 2
in C
Vn. 1
Vn. 2
Va.
Vc.
Cb.
cresc.
cresc.
cresc.
(arco)
f
(arco)
f
B
49
Fl. 1, 2
Hn. 1, 2
in C
Vn. 1
Vn. 2
Va.
Vc.
Cb.
p
(p)
p
(p)
(p)
(pp)
(pp)

54
Fl. 1, 2
Ob. 1, 2
Cl. 1, 2
in B♭
Bn. 1, 2
Hn. 1, 2
in C
Vn. 1
Vn. 2
Va.
Vc.
Cb.
59
sempre sotto voce
cresc.

130

131

C
72
Fl. 1, 2
Ob. 1, 2
Cl. 1, 2
in B♭
Bn. 1, 2
Hn. 1, 2
in C
Tpt. 1, 2
in C
A. Trb.
T. Trb.
B. Trb.
Timp.
Vn. 1
Vn. 2
Va.
Vc.
Cb.
mf
(mf)
(p)

75
Fl. 1, 2
mf
Ob. 1, 2
Cl. 1, 2
in B♭
Bn. 1, 2
Hn. 1, 2
in C
Tpt. 1, 2
in C
A. Trb.
T. Trb.
B. Trb.
Timp.
Vn. 1
Vn. 2
Va.
Vc.
Cb.

78
a 2
Fl. 1, 2
Ob. 1, 2
Cl. 1, 2
in B♭
Bn. 1, 2
1
Hn. 1, 2
in C
Tpt. 1, 2
in C
A. Trb.
T. Trb.
B. Trb.
Timp.
Vn. 1
Vn. 2
Va.
Vc.
Cb.

81
Fl. 1, 2
1
Ob. 1, 2
1
mf
Cl. 1, 2
in B♭
Bn. 1, 2
1
Hn. 1, 2
in C
Tpt. 1, 2
in C
A. Trb.
T. Trb.
B. Trb.
Timp.
Vn. 1
Vn. 2
Va.
Vc.
Cb.

84
Fl. 1, 2
Ob. 1, 2
Cl. 1, 2
in B♭
Bn. 1, 2
Hn. 1, 2
in C
mf
Tpt. 1, 2
in C
A. Trb.
T. Trb.
B. Trb.
Timp.
Vn. 1
Vn. 2
Va.
Vc.
Cb.

87
a 2
D
Fl. 1, 2
Ob. 1, 2
Cl. 1, 2
in B♭
Bn. 1, 2
Hn. 1, 2
in C
1 (solo)
(f)
Tpt. 1, 2
in C
1 (solo)
(f)
A. Trb.
T. Trb.
B. Trb.
Timp.
Vn. 1
Vn. 2
Va.
Vc.
(f)
Cb.
f

90
Fl. 1, 2
Ob. 1, 2
Cl. 1, 2
in B♭
Bn. 1, 2
Hn. 1, 2
in C
1
Tpt. 1, 2
in C
1
A. Trb.
T. Trb.
B. Trb.
Timp.
Vn. 1
(f)
Vn. 2
(f)
Va.
(f)
Vc.
Cb.

93
Fl. 1, 2
Ob. 1, 2
Cl. 1, 2
in B♭
Bn. 1, 2
Hn. 1, 2
in C
Tpt. 1, 2
in C
A. Trb.
T. Trb.
B. Trb.
Timp.
Vn. 1
Vn. 2
Va.
Vc.
Cb.
ff
mf
tr

97
Fl. 1, 2
Ob. 1, 2
Cl. 1, 2
in B♭
Bn. 1, 2
Hn. 1, 2
in C
Tpt. 1, 2
in C
A. Trb.
T. Trb.
B. Trb.
Timp.
Vn. 1
Vn. 2
Va.
Vc.
Cb.
a 2
a 2
a 2
tr

102
Fl. 1, 2
sempre ff
Ob. 1, 2
sempre ff
Cl. 1, 2
in B♭
sempre ff
Bn. 1, 2
a 2
3
sempre ff
Hn. 1, 2
in C
a 2
sempre ff
Tpt. 1, 2
in C
a 2
sempre ff
A. Trb.
T. Trb.
sempre ff
B. Trb.
sempre ff
Timp.
sempre ff
Vn. 1
sempre ff
Vn. 2
sempre ff
Va.
sempre ff
Vc.
3
sempre ff
Cb.
3
sempre ff

107
E
a 2
Fl. 1, 2
Ob. 1, 2
Cl. 1, 2
in B♭
Bn. 1, 2
a 2
Hn. 1, 2
in C
a 2
Tpt. 1, 2
in C
A. Trb.
T. Trb.
B. Trb.
Timp.
Vn. 1
p
Vn. 2
(p)
Va.
(p)
Vc.
Cb.

112
Ob. 1, 2
Bn. 1, 2
Vn. 1
Vn. 2
Va.
Vc.
Cb.
1
p
1
p
(p)
(p)
116
Ob. 1, 2
Bn. 1, 2
Vn. 1
Vn. 2
Va.
Vc.
Cb.

120
a 2
Bn. 1, 2
cresc.
Vn. 1
(cresc.)
Vn. 2
(cresc.)
Va.
cresc.
Vc.
[cresc.]
Cb.
[cresc.]

124
Cl. 1, 2
in B♭
f
Bn. 1, 2
f
Vn. 1
f
Vn. 2
f
Va.
Vc.
f
Cb.
f

128
Cl. 1, 2 in B♭
Bn. 1, 2
Vn. 1
Vn. 2
Va.
Vc.
Cb.
(cresc.)
[cresc.]
cresc.
cresc.
f
cresc.
f
f
132
Cl. 1, 2 in B♭
Bn. 1, 2
Vn. 1
Vn. 2
Va.
Vc.
Cb.
(dim.)
(dim.)

136
Ob. 1, 2
Cl. 1, 2
in B♭
Bn. 1, 2
Vn. 1
Vn. 2
Va.
Vc.
Cb.
dim.
dim.
p
p
140
Ob. 1, 2
Bn. 1, 2
Vn. 1
Vn. 2
Va.
Vc.
Cb.
p
p
p
p
p

F
144
Fl. 1, 2
Ob. 1, 2
Cl. 1, 2
in B♭
Bn. 1, 2
Hn. 1, 2
in C
Tpt. 1, 2
in C
A. Trb.
T. Trb.
B. Trb.
Timp.
Vn. 1
Vn. 2
Va.
Vc.
Cb.

147
1
[>]
Fl. 1, 2
mf
Ob. 1, 2
Cl. 1, 2
in B♭
(>)
Bn. 1, 2
a 2
Hn. 1, 2
in C
Tpt. 1, 2
in C
A. Trb.
T. Trb.
B. Trb.
Timp.
Vn. 1
Vn. 2
Va.
Vc.
Cb.
f

149

150

156
Fl. 1, 2
f
Ob. 1, 2
f
Cl. 1, 2
in B♭
(cresc.)
f
Bn. 1, 2
(cresc.)
f
a 2
Hn. 1, 2
in C
f
Tpt. 1, 2
in C
A. Trb.
T. Trb.
f
B. Trb.
f
Timp.
Vn. 1
3
f
Vn. 2
3
(cresc.)
f
Va.
3
(cresc.)
f
Vc.
f
Cb.
f

160
Fl. 1, 2
Ob. 1, 2
Cl. 1, 2
in B♭
a 2
Bn. 1, 2
Hn. 1, 2
in C
Tpt. 1, 2
in C
A. Trb.
T. Trb.
B. Trb.
Timp.
Vn. 1
Vn. 2
Va.
Vc.
Cb.
ff

153

154

184
1 (solo)
a piacere
Ob. 1, 2
G
189
Come primo
Ob. 1, 2
p
Come primo
pizz.
Vn. 1
(p)
pizz.
Vn. 2
p
pizz.
Va.
p
pizz.
Vc.
p
197
Ob. 1, 2
f
dim.
[arco]
Vn. 1
(f)
[arco]
Vn. 2
(f)
[arco]
Va.
(f)
(arco)
Vc.
(f)
(arco)
Cb.
(f)

156

157

216
Fl. 1, 2
Ob. 1, 2
Cl. 1, 2
in B♭
Bn. 1, 2
Hn. 1, 2
in C
Tpt. 1, 2
in C
A. Trb.
T. Trb.
B. Trb.
Timp.
Vn. 1
Vn. 2
Va.
Vc.
Cb.
ff
(f cresc.)

159

225
Fl. 1, 2
Ob. 1, 2
Cl. 1, 2
in B♭
Bn. 1, 2
a 2
Hn. 1, 2
in C
a 2
Tpt. 1, 2
in C
a 2
A. Trb.
T. Trb.
B. Trb.
Timp.
Vn. 1
Vn. 2
Va.
Vc.
Cb.

161

I
234
a 2
Fl. 1, 2
1
p
Ob. 1, 2
1
p
Cl. 1, 2
in B♭
Bn. 1, 2
Hn. 1, 2
in C
a 2
Tpt. 1, 2
in C
a 2
A. Trb.
T. Trb.
B. Trb.
Timp.
Vn. 1
p
Vn. 2
(p)
Va.
(p)
Vc.
pizz.
(p)
Cb.

163

L
246
Cl. 1, 2 in B♭
Hn. 1, 2 in C
1 [solo]
p
Vn. 1
pp
Vn. 2
Va.
Vc.
arco
(pp)
Cb.
250
Cl. 1, 2 in B♭
1
p
Hn. 1, 2 in C
p
Vn. 1
Vn. 2
Va.
pp
3
3
3
Vc.
(p)
Cb.

165

262
Fl. 1, 2
Ob. 1, 2
Cl. 1, 2
in B♭
Bn. 1, 2
Hn. 1, 2
in C
Tpt. 1, 2
in C
A. Trb.
T. Trb.
B. Trb.
Timp.
Vn. 1
Vn. 2
Va.
Vc.
Cb.
p
(p)

167

268
a 2
Fl. 1, 2
sfp
Ob. 1, 2
sfp
p
Cl. 1, 2
in B♭
sfp
p
Bn. 1, 2
1
Hn. 1, 2
in C
3
Tpt. 1, 2
in C
A. Trb.
T. Trb.
B. Trb.
Timp.
Vn. 1
sf
(p)
Vn. 2
sf
(p)
Va.
3
3
(p)
Vc.
(sf)
p
Cb.
(sf)

271
Fl. 1, 2
Ob. 1, 2
Cl. 1, 2
in B♭
1
Bn. 1, 2
Hn. 1, 2
in C
Tpt. 1, 2
in C
A. Trb.
T. Trb.
B. Trb.
Timp.
Vn. 1
Vn. 2
Va.
Vc.
Cb.
p

274
8va
Fl. 1, 2
p
Ob. 1, 2
Cl. 1, 2
in B♭
1
Bn. 1, 2
p
Hn. 1, 2
in C
1
p
Tpt. 1, 2
in C
A. Trb.
T. Trb.
B. Trb.
Timp.
Vn. 1
Vn. 2
Va.
Vc.
Cb.

277
Fl. 1, 2
Ob. 1, 2
Cl. 1, 2
in B♭
Bn. 1, 2
Hn. 1, 2
in C
Tpt. 1, 2
in C
A. Trb.
T. Trb.
B. Trb.
tr
Timp.
pp
Vn. 1
Vn. 2
Va.
Vc.
Cb.

281
8va
a 2
a 2
a 2
(tr)
Fl. 1, 2
Ob. 1, 2
Cl. 1, 2 in B♭
Bn. 1, 2
Hn. 1, 2 in C
Tpt. 1, 2 in C
A. Trb.
T. Trb.
B. Trb.
Timp.
Vn. 1
Vn. 2
Va.
Vc.
Cb.

285
Fl. 1, 2
Ob. 1, 2
Cl. 1, 2 in B♭
Bn. 1, 2
Hn. 1, 2 in C
Tpt. 1, 2 in C
A. Trb. T. Trb.
p
B. Trb.
p
Timp
Vn. 1
Vn. 2
Va.
Vc.
Cb.

289
Fl. 1, 2
Ob. 1, 2
Cl. 1, 2 in B♭
Bn. 1, 2
Hn. 1, 2 in C
a 2
[cresc.]
Tpt. 1, 2 in C
a 2
[cresc.]
A. Trb.
T. Trb.
(cresc.)
B. Trb.
(cresc.)
Timp.
Vn. 1
cresc.
Vn. 2
(cresc.)
Va.
cresc.
Vc.
[cresc.]
Cb.
[cresc.]

175

297
Fl. 1, 2
Ob. 1, 2
Cl. 1, 2
in B♭
Bn. 1, 2
Hn. 1, 2
in C
a 2
Tpt. 1, 2
in C
a 2
A. Trb.
T. Trb.
B. Trb.
Timp.
Vn. 1
sempre ff
Vn. 2
sempre ff
Va.
sempre ff
Vc.
sempre ff
Cb.
sempre ff

301
Fl. 1, 2
Ob. 1, 2
Cl. 1, 2 in B♭
Bn. 1, 2
Hn. 1, 2 in C
sf
Tpt. 1, 2 in C
sf
A. Trb. T. Trb.
sf
B. Trb.
sf
Timp.
tr
[sempre] ff
(ff)
Vn. 1
Vn. 2
Va.
Vc.
Cb.

305
Fl. 1, 2
Ob. 1, 2
Cl. 1, 2
in B♭
Bn. 1, 2
Hn. 1, 2
in C
Tpt. 1, 2
in C
A. Trb.
T. Trb.
B. Trb.
Timp.
Vn. 1
Vn. 2
Va.
Vc.
Cb.
a 2
a 2
sf
sf
sf
sf

179

314
Fl. 1, 2
Ob. 1, 2
Cl. 1, 2
in B♭
Bn. 1, 2
(a 2)
Hn. 1, 2
in C
(a 2)
Tpt. 1, 2
in C
A. Trb.
T. Trb.
B. Trb.
tr
Timp.
Vn. 1
Vn. 2
Va.
Vc.
Cb.

317
Fl. 1, 2
Ob. 1, 2
Cl. 1, 2
in B♭
Bn. 1, 2
Hn. 1, 2
in C
Tpt. 1, 2
in C
A. Trb.
T. Trb.
B. Trb.
(tr)
Timp.
(cresc.)
Vn. 1
Vn. 2
Va.
Vc.
Cb.

320
Fl. 1, 2
Ob. 1, 2
Cl. 1, 2
in B♭
Bn. 1, 2
Hn. 1, 2
in C
Tpt. 1, 2
in C
A. Trb.
T. Trb.
B. Trb.
(tr)
Timp.
Vn. 1
Vn. 2
Va.
Vc.
Cb.

324
a 2
Fl. 1, 2
ff
Ob. 1, 2
a 2
Cl. 1, 2
in B♭
Bn. 1, 2
Hn. 1, 2
in C
Tpt. 1, 2
in C
A. Trb.
T. Trb.
B. Trb.
Timp.
tr
Vn. 1
Vn. 2
Va.
Vc.
Cb.

328
a 2
Fl. 1, 2
Ob. 1, 2
Cl. 1, 2
in B♭
Bn. 1, 2
Hn. 1, 2
in C
Tpt. 1, 2
in C
A. Trb.
T. Trb.
B. Trb.
Timp.
Vn. 1
Vn. 2
Va.
Vc.
Cb.

Symphony in A Minor (1876)

INSTRUMENTS

Flute (Fl.) 1, 2
Oboe (Ob.) 1, 2
Clarinet (Cl.) 1, 2
Bassoon (Bn.) 1, 2

Horn (Hn.) 1, 2
Trumpet (Tpt.) 1, 2
Alto Trombone (A. Trb.)
Tenor Trombone (T. Trb.)
Bass Trombone (B. Trb.)

Timpani (Timp.)

Violin (Vn.) 1
Violin (Vn.) 2
Viola (Va.)
Violoncello (Vc.)
Contrabass (Cb.)

I

10
Vn. 1
Vn. 2
Va.
Vc.
Cb.
pp
17
Fl. 1, 2
Ob. 1, 2
Cl. 1, 2 in A
Bn. 1, 2
1
a 2
pp
Vn. 1
Vn. 2
Va.
Vc.
Cb.

23
Fl. 1, 2
cresc.
fz
Ob. 1, 2
cresc.
fz
Cl. 1, 2 in A
cresc.
fz
p
Bn. 1, 2
cresc.
fz
p
Hn. 1, 2 in C
fz
p
Tpt. 1, 2 in D
1
fz
A. Trb. T. Trb.
fz
B. Trb.
fz
Timp.
Vn. 1
cresc.
fz
p
Vn. 2
cresc.
fz
p
Va.
cresc.
fz
p
Vc.
cresc.
fz
p
Cb.
cresc.
fz
p

28
a 2
Fl. 1, 2
p
cresc.
Ob. 1, 2
p
cresc.
Cl. 1, 2
in A
cresc.
Bn. 1, 2
cresc.
Hn. 1, 2
in C
p
Tpt. 1, 2
in D
A. Trb.
T. Trb.
B. Trb.
Timp.
Vn. 1
cresc.
Vn. 2
cresc.
Va.
cresc.
Vc.
cresc.
Cb.
cresc.

A
34
Fl. 1, 2
Ob. 1, 2
Cl. 1, 2
in A
Bn. 1, 2
Hn. 1, 2
in C
a 2
Tpt. 1, 2
in D
a 2
A. Trb.
T. Trb.
B. Trb.
Timp.
Vn. 1
Vn. 2
Va.
Vc.
Cb.
fz
p
ff

40
Fl. 1, 2
Ob. 1, 2
Cl. 1, 2 in A
Bn. 1, 2
Hn. 1, 2 in C
Tpt. 1, 2 in D
A. Trb.
T. Trb.
B. Trb.
Timp.
Vn. 1
Vn. 2
Va.
Vc.
Cb.

46
Fl. 1, 2
a 2
Ob. 1, 2
Cl. 1, 2 in A
Bn. 1, 2
a 2
Hn. 1, 2 in C
a 2
a 2
Tpt. 1, 2 in D
A. Trb. T. Trb.
B. Trb.
Timp.
Vn. 1
Vn. 2
Va.
Vc.
Cb.

52
a 2
Fl. 1, 2
Ob. 1, 2
Cl. 1, 2
in A
Bn. 1, 2
Hn. 1, 2
in C
Tpt. 1, 2
in D
A. Trb.
T. Trb.
B. Trb.
Timp.
Vn. 1
Vn. 2
Va.
Vc.
Cb.

58
B
Fl. 1, 2
Ob. 1, 2
Cl. 1, 2
in A
Bn. 1, 2
Hn. 1, 2
in C
Tpt. 1, 2
in D
A. Trb.
T. Trb.
B. Trb.
Timp.
Vn. 1
Vn. 2
Va.
Vc.
Cb.
solo
a 2

196

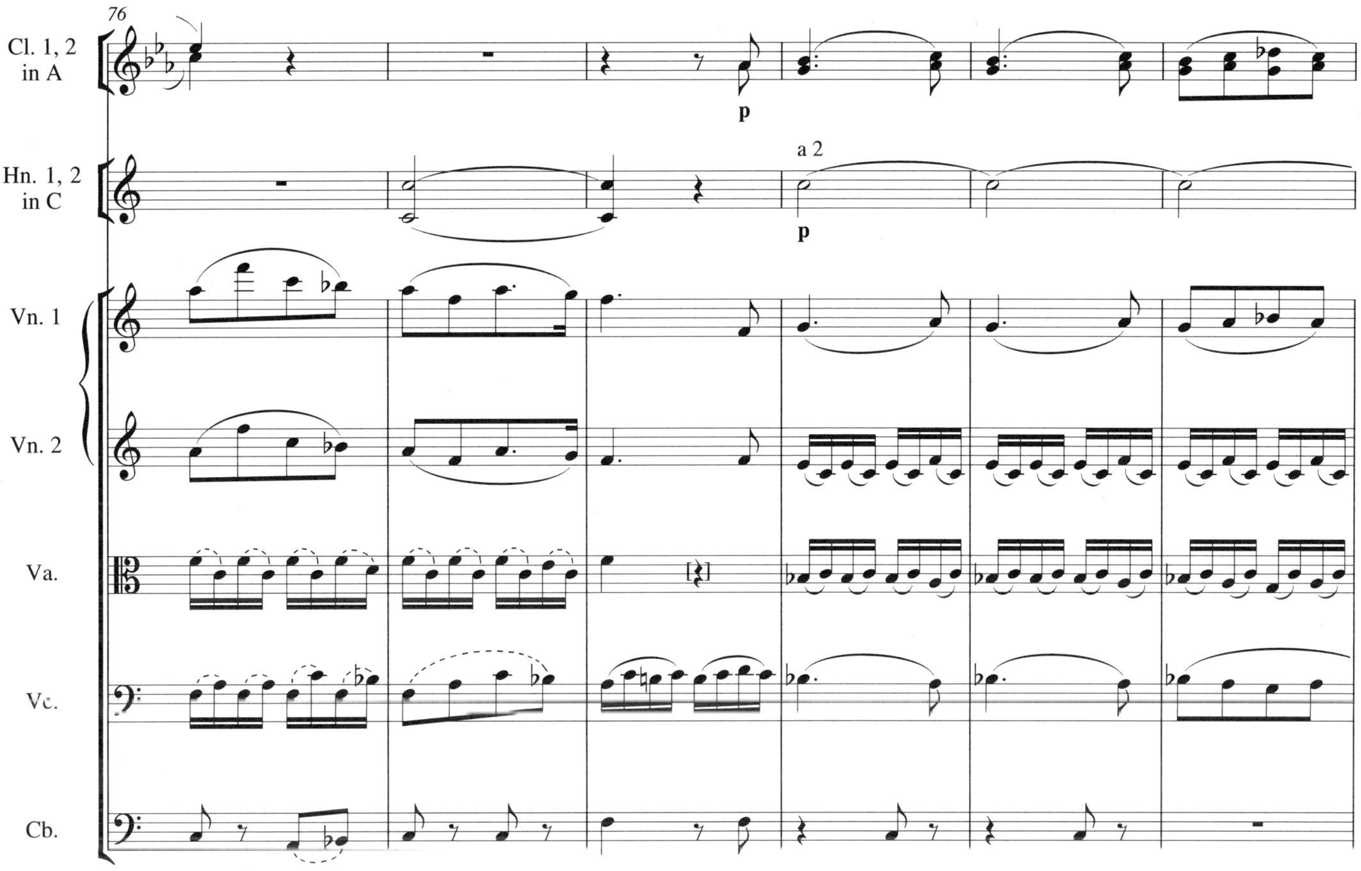
76
Cl. 1, 2
in A
p
Hn. 1, 2
in C
a 2
p
Vn. 1
Vn. 2
Va.
Vc.
Cb.

82
Cl. 1, 2
in A
[1]
Bn. 1, 2
p
Hn. 1, 2
in C
a 2
Vn. 1
Vn. 2
Va.
Vc.
Cb.

88
Fl. 1, 2
1
p
Ob. 1, 2
Cl. 1, 2
in A
[1]
Bn. 1, 2
a 2
Hn. 1, 2
in C
Tpt. 1, 2
in D
A. Trb.
T. Trb.
B. Trb.
Timp.
Vn. 1
Vn. 2
Va.
Vc.
Cb.

94
Fl. 1, 2
[cresc.]
Ob. 1, 2
p
cresc.
Cl. 1, 2
in A
cresc.
Bn. 1, 2
cresc.
Hn. 1, 2
in C
a 2
cresc.
Tpt. 1, 2
in D
A. Trb.
T. Trb.
B. Trb.
p [cresc.]
Timp.
p
[cresc.]
Vn. 1
cresc.
Vn. 2
cresc.
Va.
cresc.
Vc.
cresc.
Cb.
cresc.

100
1
a 2
Fl. 1, 2
Ob. 1, 2
[♭]
a 2
Cl. 1, 2
in A
Bn. 1, 2
a 2
Hn. 1, 2
in C
Tpt. 1, 2
in D
p [cresc.]
A. Trb.
T. Trb.
B. Trb.
Timp.
Vn. 1
Vn. 2
Va.
Vc.
Cb.

106
Fl. 1, 2
a 2
ff
Ob. 1, 2
[a 2]
ff
Cl. 1, 2
in A
a 2
ff
Bn. 1, 2
a 2
ff
Hn. 1, 2
in C
ff
Tpt. 1, 2
in D
ff
A. Trb.
T. Trb.
B. Trb.
Timp.
Vn. 1
ff
Vn. 2
ff
Va.
ff
Vc.
ff
Cb.
ff

112
C
a 2
Fl. 1, 2
p
[a 2]
Ob. 1, 2
p
a 2
Cl. 1, 2
in A
a 2
Bn. 1, 2
p
Hn. 1, 2
in C
Tpt. 1, 2
in D
A. Trb.
T. Trb.
B. Trb.
Timp.
Vn. 1
p
Vn. 2
p
Va.
p
Vc.
p
Cb.
p

119
Fl. 1, 2
Ob. 1, 2
Cl. 1, 2 in A
Bn. 1, 2
Hn. 1, 2 in C
a 2
Tpt. 1, 2 in D
A. Trb.
T. Trb.
B. Trb.
Timp.
Vn. 1
Vn. 2
Va.
Vc.
Cb.
p
pp
ff
f

127
1.
[a 2]
a 2
[1]
Fl. 1, 2
Ob. 1, 2
Cl. 1, 2
in A
Bn. 1, 2
Hn. 1, 2
in C
Tpt. 1, 2
in D
A. Trb.
T. Trb.
B. Trb.
Timp.
Vn. 1
Vn. 2
Va.
Vc.
Cb.
f
p
pp

134
2.
Fl. 1, 2
Ob. 1, 2
Cl. 1, 2
in A
Bn. 1, 2
Hn. 1, 2
in C
Tpt. 1, 2
in D
A. Trb.
T. Trb.
B. Trb.
Timp.
2.
Vn. 1
Vn. 2
Va.
Vc.
Cb.
pp

140
Fl. 1, 2
Ob. 1, 2
Cl. 1, 2 in A
Bn. 1, 2
Hn. 1, 2 in C
Tpt. 1, 2 in D
A. Trb. T. Trb.
B. Trb.
Timp.
Vn. 1
cresc.
Vn. 2
cresc.
Va.
cresc.
Vc.
cresc.
Cb.
cresc.

146
D
[1]
Fl. 1, 2
Ob. 1, 2
Cl. 1, 2
in A
a 2
Bn. 1, 2
[cresc.]
Hn. 1, 2
in C
a 2
Tpt. 1, 2
in D
A. Trb.
T. Trb.
B. Trb.
Timp.
Vn. 1
Vn. 2
Va.
Vc.
Cb.
f

[1]
152
Fl. 1, 2
Ob. 1, 2
Cl. 1, 2
in A
Bn. 1, 2
Hn. 1, 2
in C
a 2
Tpt. 1, 2
in D
A. Trb.
T. Trb.
B. Trb.
Timp.
Vn. 1
Vn. 2
Va.
Vc.
Cb.

158
Fl. 1, 2
Ob. 1, 2
Cl. 1, 2 in A
Bn. 1, 2
Hn. 1, 2 in C
Tpt. 1, 2 in D
A. Trb. T. Trb.
B. Trb.
Timp.
Vn. 1
Vn. 2
Va.
Vc.
Cb.

163
a 2
Fl. 1, 2
Ob. 1, 2
Cl. 1, 2
in A
Bn. 1, 2
Hn. 1, 2
in C
Tpt. 1, 2
in D
A. Trb.
T. Trb.
B. Trb.
Timp.
Vn. 1
Vn. 2
Va.
Vc.
Cb.
ff

169
Fl. 1, 2
Ob. 1, 2
Cl. 1, 2
in A
Bn. 1, 2
Hn. 1, 2
in C
Tpt. 1, 2
in D
A. Trb.
T. Trb.
B. Trb.
Timp.
Vn. 1
Vn. 2
Va.
Vc.
Cb.
[1]

E
175
Fl. 1, 2
Ob. 1, 2
Cl. 1, 2
in A
Bn. 1, 2
Hn. 1, 2
in C
Tpt. 1, 2
in D
A. Trb.
T. Trb.
B. Trb.
Timp.
Vn. 1
Vn. 2
Va.
Vc.
Cb.
[1]
a 2
[a 2]
p
pp

213

194
Fl. 1, 2
Ob. 1, 2
Cl. 1, 2
in A
Bn. 1, 2
Hn. 1, 2
in C
Tpt. 1, 2
in D
A. Trb.
T. Trb.
B. Trb.
Timp.
Vn. 1
Vn. 2
Va.
Vc.
Cb.
a 2
sf

F
202
Fl. 1, 2
[a 2]
Ob. 1, 2
Cl. 1, 2 in A
Bn. 1, 2
Hn. 1, 2 in C
a 2
Tpt. 1, 2 in D
A. Trb.
T. Trb.
B. Trb.
Timp.
Vn. 1
Vn. 2
Va.
Vc.
Cb.

216

215
Fl. 1, 2
Ob. 1, 2
Cl. 1, 2
in A
a 2
Bn. 1, 2
Hn. 1, 2
in C
ff
Tpt. 1, 2
in D
A. Trb.
T. Trb.
B. Trb.
Timp.
Vn. 1
Vn. 2
Va.
Vc.
Cb.

218

229
Fl. 1, 2
decresc.
Ob. 1, 2
decresc.
Cl. 1, 2
in A
Bn. 1, 2
decresc.
Hn. 1, 2
in C
p [decresc.]
Tpt. 1, 2
in D
A. Trb.
T. Trb.
B. Trb.
Timp.
Vn. 1
decresc.
pizz.
arco
pp
Vn. 2
decresc.
pizz.
Va.
decresc.
pizz.
Vc.
decresc.
pizz.
Cb.
decresc.
pizz.

G
237
Fl. 1, 2
Ob. 1, 2
Cl. 1, 2
in A
Bn. 1, 2
Hn. 1, 2
in C
Tpt. 1, 2
in D
A. Trb.
T. Trb.
B. Trb.
Timp.
Vn. 1
Vn. 2
arco
pp
Va.
arco
pp
Vc.
arco
pp
Cb.
arco
pp

243
Fl. 1, 2
1
pp
[a 2]
Ob. 1, 2
1
pp
Cl. 1, 2
in A
pp
Bn. 1, 2
pp
Hn. 1, 2
in C
Tpt. 1, 2
in D
A. Trb.
T. Trb.
B. Trb.
Timp.
Vn. 1
Vn. 2
Va.
Vc.
Cb.

249
[a 2]
Fl. 1, 2
Ob. 1, 2
Cl. 1, 2
in A
Bn. 1, 2
Hn. 1, 2
in C
Tpt. 1, 2
in D
A. Trb.
T. Trb.
B. Trb.
Timp.
Vn. 1
Vn. 2
Va.
Vc.
Cb.
cresc.
sf
p

255
[a 2]
Fl. 1, 2
p
cresc.
sf
Ob. 1, 2
p
cresc.
sf
Cl. 1, 2
in A
cresc.
sf
Bn. 1, 2
cresc.
sf
Hn. 1, 2
in C
p
sf
Tpt. 1, 2
in D
sf
A. Trb.
T. Trb.
B. Trb.
Timp.
Vn. 1
cresc.
sf
Vn. 2
cresc.
sf
Va.
cresc.
sf
Vc.
cresc.
sf
Cb.
cresc.
sf

261
Fl. 1, 2
a 2
Ob. 1, 2
a 2
Cl. 1, 2
in A
[a 2]
Bn. 1, 2
Hn. 1, 2
in C
a 2
Tpt. 1, 2
in D
a 2
A. Trb.
T. Trb.
f
B. Trb.
f
Timp.
f
tr
Vn. 1
Vn. 2
Va.
Vc.
Cb.

H
267
Fl. 1, 2
pp
Ob. 1, 2
Cl. 1, 2
in A
Bn. 1, 2
a 2
p
Hn. 1, 2
in C
Tpt. 1, 2
in D
A. Trb.
T. Trb.
B. Trb.
Timp.
(tr)
Vn. 1
p
pp
Vn. 2
p
pp
Va.
p
pp
Vc.
p
Cb.
p

274
Fl. 1, 2
a 2
Bn. 1, 2
Vn. 1
Vn. 2
Va.
Vc.
Cb.

280
Cl. 1, 2
in A
p
Bn. 1, 2
Hn. 1, 2
in C
p
Vn. 1
Vn. 2
Va.
Vc.
Cb.

286
Fl. 1, 2
Ob. 1, 2
Cl. 1, 2
in A
1
Bn. 1, 2
Hn. 1, 2
in C
Tpt. 1, 2
in D
A. Trb.
T. Trb.
B. Trb.
Timp.
Vn. 1
Vn. 2
Va.
Vc.
Cb.

292
Fl. 1, 2
Ob. 1, 2
Cl. 1, 2
in A
Bn. 1, 2
Hn. 1, 2
in C
Tpt. 1, 2
in D
A. Trb.
T. Trb.
B. Trb.
Timp.
Vn. 1
Vn. 2
Va.
Vc.
Cb.

298
Fl. 1, 2
Ob. 1, 2
Cl. 1, 2
in A
Bn. 1, 2
Hn. 1, 2
in C
Tpt. 1, 2
in D
A. Trb.
T. Trb.
B. Trb.
Timp.
Vn. 1
Vn. 2
Va.
Vc.
Cb.
a 2
p

304
Fl. 1, 2
Ob. 1, 2
Cl. 1, 2
in A
Bn. 1, 2
Hn. 1, 2
in C
Tpt. 1, 2
in D
p
A. Trb.
T. Trb.
B. Trb.
tr
Timp.
p
Vn. 1
Vn. 2
Va.
Vc.
Cb.

310
Fl. 1, 2
Ob. 1, 2
Cl. 1, 2
in A
Bn. 1, 2
a 2
Hn. 1, 2
in C
Tpt. 1, 2
in D
A. Trb.
T. Trb.
B. Trb.
Timp.
Vn. 1
Vn. 2
Va.
Vc.
Cb.

I
316
Fl. 1, 2
Ob. 1, 2
Cl. 1, 2
in A
Bn. 1, 2
Hn. 1, 2
in C
Tpt. 1, 2
in D
A. Trb.
T. Trb.
B. Trb.
Timp.
Vn. 1
Vn. 2
Va.
Vc.
Cb.
a 2
ff
p
tr

233

234

235

236

237

356
Fl. 1, 2
a 2
ff
Ob. 1, 2
[a 2]
ff
Cl. 1, 2
in A
ff
a 2
Bn. 1, 2
ff
a 2
Hn. 1, 2
in C
ff
Tpt. 1, 2
in D
ff
a 2
A. Trb.
T. Trb.
ff
B. Trb.
ff
Timp.
ff
Vn. 1
Vn. 2
Va.
Vc.
Cb.

II

8
Cl. 1, 2 in A
Bn. 1, 2
Vn. 1
cantabile
Vn. 2
pizz.
Va.
pizz.
Vc.
pizz.
Cb.
pizz.
15
Cl. 1, 2 in A
Bn. 1, 2
1
Hn. 1, 2 in D
1
pp
Vn. 1
Vn. 2
arco
Va.
arco
Vc.
arco
Cb.
arco

A
22
Fl. 1, 2
Ob. 1, 2
Cl. 1, 2
in A
Bn. 1, 2
Hn. 1, 2
in D
a 2
Tpt. 1, 2
in D
A. Trb.
T. Trb.
B. Trb.
Timp.
Vn. 1
Vn. 2
Va.
Vc.
Cb.
pp
pizz.
[arco]

29
Fl. 1, 2
Ob. 1, 2
Cl. 1, 2
in A
Bn. 1, 2
Hn. 1, 2
in D
Tpt. 1, 2
in D
A. Trb.
T. Trb.
B. Trb.
Timp.
Vn. 1
Vn. 2
Va.
Vc.
Cb.
[arco]
arco

B
36
Fl. 1, 2
Ob. 1, 2
Cl. 1, 2
in A
Bn. 1, 2
Hn. 1, 2
in D
Tpt. 1, 2
in D
A. Trb.
T. Trb.
B. Trb.
Timp.
Vn. 1
Vn. 2
Va.
Vc.
Cb.
cresc.
[cresc.]
p
pp
tr

42
Fl. 1, 2
Ob. 1, 2
Cl. 1, 2 in A
Bn. 1, 2
[1] solo
p
Hn. 1, 2 in D
Tpt. 1, 2 in D
A. Trb.
T. Trb.
B. Trb.
Timp.
tr
Vn. 1
Vn. 2
Va.
Vc.
Cb.

47
Fl. 1, 2
Ob. 1, 2
Cl. 1, 2
in A
Bn. 1, 2
a 2
Hn. 1, 2
in D
Tpt. 1, 2
in D
A. Trb.
T. Trb.
B. Trb.
Timp.
Vn. 1
Vn. 2
Va.
Vc.
Cb.
[1]
1
p

52
Fl. 1, 2
Ob. 1, 2
Cl. 1, 2
in A
Bn. 1, 2
pp
Hn. 1, 2
in D
Tpt. 1, 2
in D
A. Trb.
T. Trb.
B. Trb.
Timp.
Vn. 1
pp
Vn. 2
pp
Va.
pp
Vc.
pp
Cb.

C
57
Fl. 1, 2
Ob. 1, 2
Cl. 1, 2
in A
Bn. 1, 2
Hn. 1, 2
in D
Tpt. 1, 2
in D
A. Trb.
T. Trb.
B. Trb.
Timp.
Vn. 1
Vn. 2
Va.
Vc.
Cb.
a 2
pp
sf
ff
tr

*See Critical Notes.

70
Fl. 1, 2
Ob. 1, 2
Cl. 1, 2
in A
Bn. 1, 2
Hn. 1, 2
in D
Tpt. 1, 2
in D
A. Trb.
T. Trb.
B. Trb.
Timp.
Vn. 1
Vn. 2
Va.
Vc.
Cb.
1
p
tr

250

79
Fl. 1, 2
Ob. 1, 2
Cl. 1, 2
in A
Bn. 1, 2
Hn. 1, 2
in D
Tpt. 1, 2
in D
A. Trb.
T. Trb.
B. Trb.
Timp.
Vn. 1
Vn. 2
Va.
Vc.
Cb.
sf
p
pp
1
[1]

D
86
Fl. 1, 2
Ob. 1, 2
Cl. 1, 2 in A
Bn. 1, 2
Hn. 1, 2 in D
Tpt. 1, 2 in D
A. Trb.
T. Trb.
B. Trb.
Timp.
Vn. 1
Vn. 2
Va.
Vc.
Cb.
pizz.
pizz.
pizz.

93
Fl. 1, 2
Ob. 1, 2
Cl. 1, 2
in A
Bn. 1, 2
1
Hn. 1, 2
in D
Tpt. 1, 2
in D
A. Trb.
T. Trb.
B. Trb.
Timp.
Vn. 1
Vn. 2
Va.
Vc.
Cb.

100
Fl. 1, 2
Ob. 1, 2
Cl. 1, 2 in A
Bn. 1, 2
Hn. 1, 2 in D
Tpt. 1, 2 in D
A. Trb. T. Trb.
B. Trb.
Timp.
Vn. 1
Vn. 2
Va.
Vc.
Cb.
arco
arco
arco
p

E
107
Fl. 1, 2
Ob. 1, 2
[1] solo
Cl. 1, 2 in A
[1] solo
Bn. 1, 2
Hn. 1, 2 in D
Tpt. 1, 2 in D
A. Trb. T. Trb.
B. Trb.
Timp.
Vn. 1
Vn. 2
Va.
Vc.
Cb.
pp

256

124
Fl. 1, 2
Ob. 1, 2
Cl. 1, 2
in A
Bn. 1, 2
p
Hn. 1, 2
in D
1
p
Tpt. 1, 2
in D
A. Trb.
T. Trb.
B. Trb.
Timp.
Vn. 1
Vn. 2
[arco]
Va.
[arco]
Vc.
[arco]
Cb.

129
F
Fl. 1, 2
Ob. 1, 2
Cl. 1, 2
in A
Bn. 1, 2
Hn. 1, 2
in D
Tpt. 1, 2
in D
A. Trb.
T. Trb.
B. Trb.
Timp.
Vn. 1
Vn. 2
Va.
Vc.
Cb.
a 2
[arco]
ff

135
Fl. 1, 2
Ob. 1, 2
Cl. 1, 2 in A
[a 2]
Bn. 1, 2
[a 2]
Hn. 1, 2 in D
Tpt. 1, 2 in D
A. Trb.
T. Trb.
a 2
B. Trb.
Timp.
tr
Vn. 1
Vn. 2
Va.
Vc.
Cb.

140
Fl. 1, 2
Ob. 1, 2
Cl. 1, 2
in A
Bn. 1, 2
Hn. 1, 2
in D
Tpt. 1, 2
in D
A. Trb.
T. Trb.
B. Trb.
Timp.
Vn. 1
Vn. 2
Va.
Vc.
Cb.
a 2
a 2
1
1
1
p
p
p
p
p
p
p
p
tr
tr
3
3
3

145
Fl. 1, 2
Ob. 1, 2
[1]
p
Cl. 1, 2
in A
Bn. 1, 2
Hn. 1, 2
in D
Tpt. 1, 2
in D
p
A. Trb.
T. Trb.
B. Trb.
Timp.
Vn. 1
Vn. 2
Va.
Vc.
Cb.

149
Fl. 1, 2
Ob. 1, 2
Cl. 1, 2
in A
Bn. 1, 2
Hn. 1, 2
in D
Tpt. 1, 2
in D
A. Trb.
T. Trb.
B. Trb.
Timp.
Vn. 1
Vn. 2
Va.
Vc.
Cb.

263

163
a 2
Fl. 1, 2
[a 2]
Ob. 1, 2
a 2
Cl. 1, 2
in A
[a 2]
Bn. 1, 2
Hn. 1, 2
in D
Tpt. 1, 2
in D
A. Trb.
T. Trb.
B. Trb.
Timp.
Vn. 1
Vn. 2
Va.
Vc.
Cb.

170
Fl. 1, 2
Ob. 1, 2
Cl. 1, 2
in A
Bn. 1, 2
[a 2]
Hn. 1, 2
in D
Tpt. 1, 2
in D
A. Trb.
T. Trb.
B. Trb.
Timp.
tr
tr
Vn. 1
Vn. 2
Va.
Vc.
Cb.

266

182
Fl. 1, 2
1
p
Ob. 1, 2
Cl. 1, 2
in A
Bn. 1, 2
Hn. 1, 2
in D
Tpt. 1, 2
in D
A. Trb.
T. Trb.
B. Trb.
Timp.
Vn. 1
p
Vn. 2
p
Va.
p
Vc.
p
Cb.
p

188
Fl. 1, 2
Ob. 1, 2
Cl. 1, 2
in A
Bn. 1, 2
Hn. 1, 2
in D
Tpt. 1, 2
in D
A. Trb.
T. Trb.
B. Trb.
Timp.
Vn. 1
Vn. 2
Va.
Vc.
Cb.
pp
p
[1]
tr

III

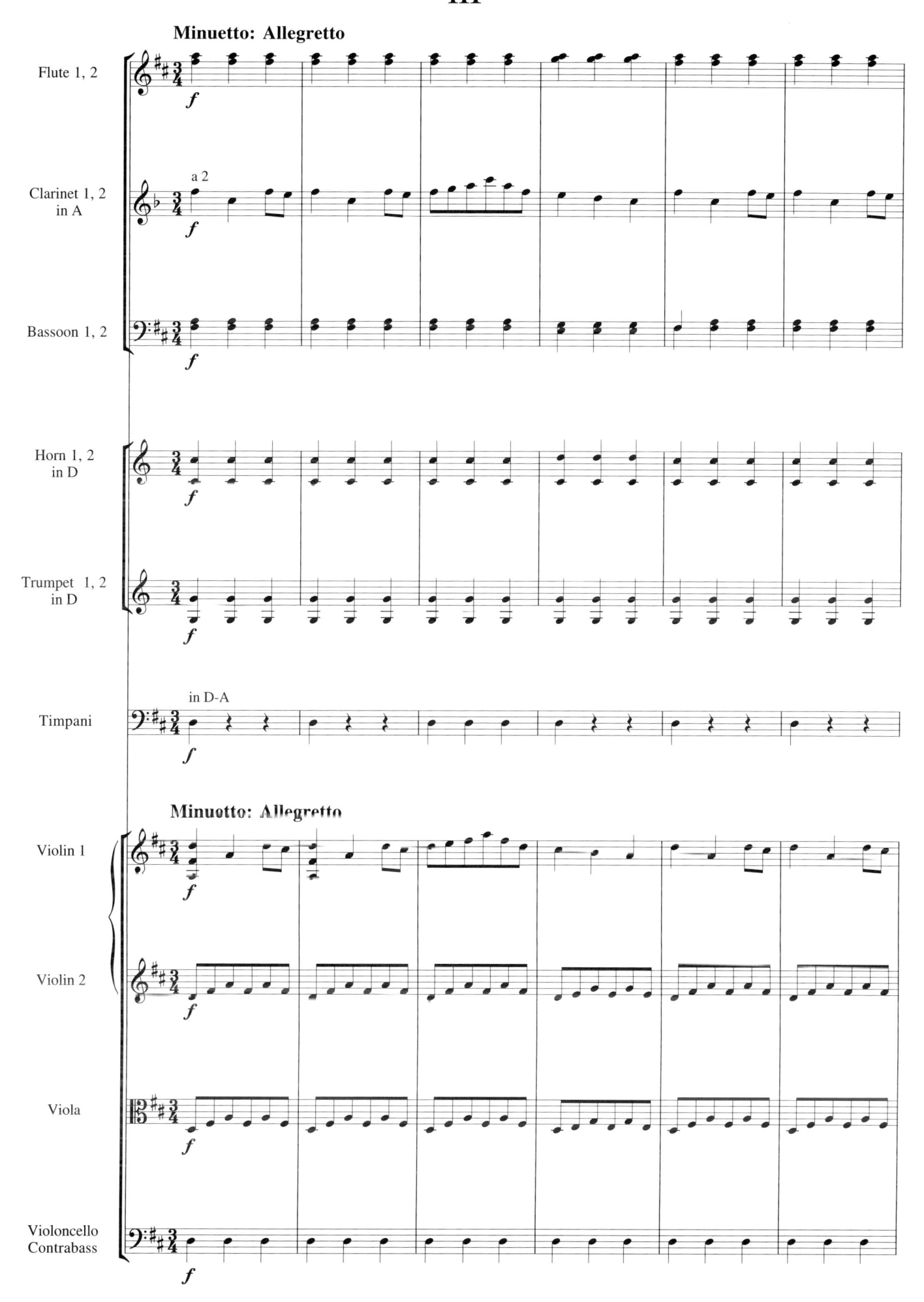

Minuetto: Allegretto

7
[a 2]
a 2
Fl. 1, 2
Cl. 1, 2
in A
Bn. 1, 2
Hn. 1, 2
in D
Tpt. 1, 2
in D
Timp.
Vn. 1
Vn. 2
Va.
Vc.
Cb.
cresc.
12
[1]

271

27
Fl. 1, 2
[a 2]
Cl. 1, 2 in A
Bn. 1, 2
Hn. 1, 2 in D
Tpt. 1, 2 in D
Timp.
Vn. 1
Vn. 2
Va.
Vc. Cb.
32
[a 2]
p
cresc.
a 2
p cresc.

37
Fl. 1, 2
Cl. 1, 2 in A
Bn. 1, 2
Hn. 1, 2 in D
Tpt. 1, 2 in D
Timp.
Vn. 1
Vn. 2
Va.
Vc. Cb.
a 2
[a 2]
42
1. [3.]
2.
Trio
pizz.
[Fine]

47
Fl. 1, 2
Cl. 1, 2 in A
Bn. 1, 2
Hn. 1, 2 in D
pp
Tpt. 1, 2 in D
Vn. 1
Vn. 2
Va.
Vc. Cb.
52
Fl. 1, 2
p
Cl. 1, 2 in A
p
Bn. 1, 2
p
Hn. 1, 2 in D
p
Tpt. 1, 2 in D
p
Vn. 1
Vn. 2
Va.
Vc. Cb.

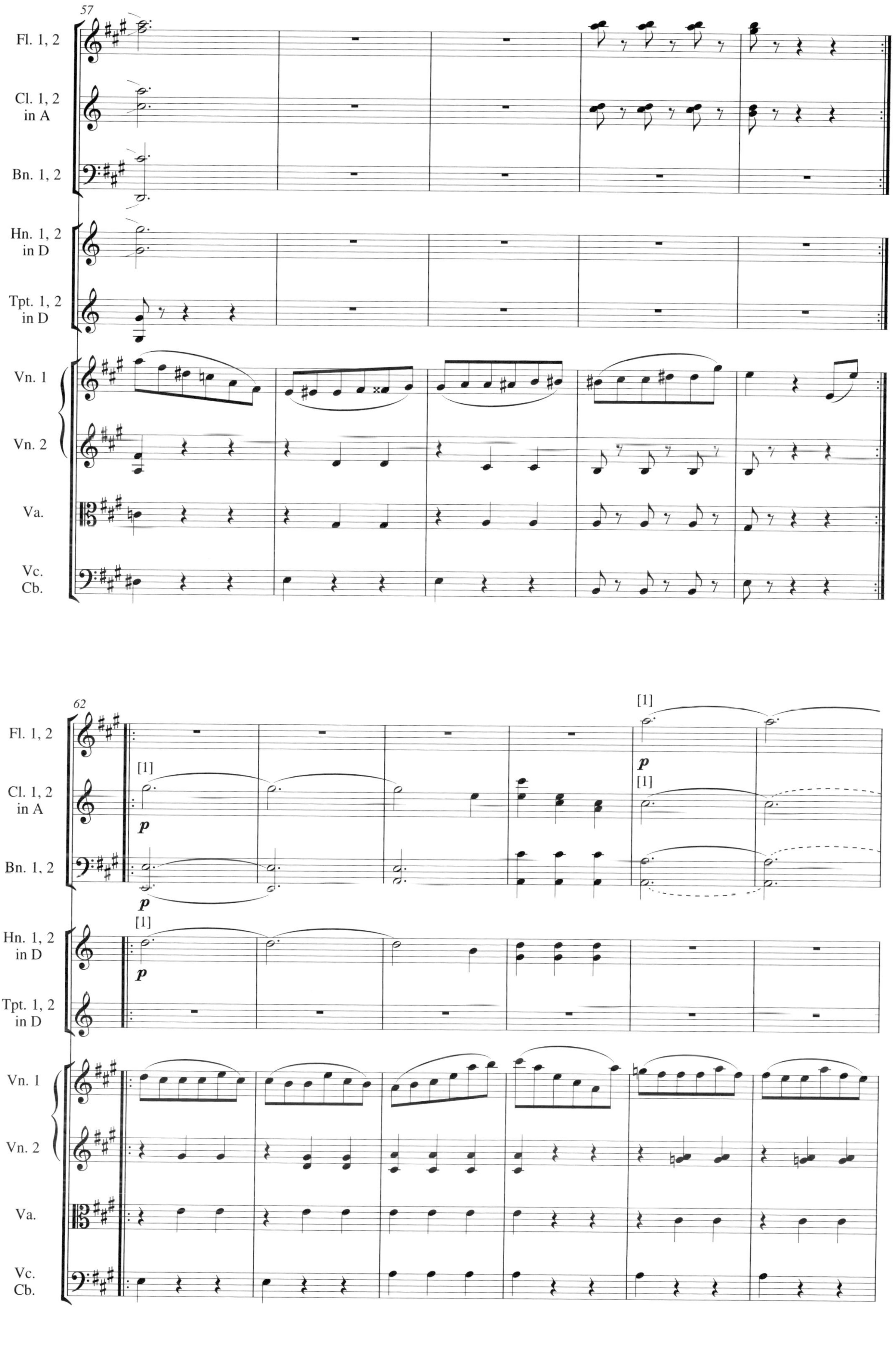
57
Fl. 1, 2
Cl. 1, 2
in A
Bn. 1, 2
Hn. 1, 2
in D
Tpt. 1, 2
in D
Vn. 1
Vn. 2
Va.
Vc.
Cb.
62
[1]
p

Minuetto D.C.

IV

4
a 2
Fl. 1, 2
[a 2]
Ob. 1, 2
Cl. 1, 2 in A
Bn. 1, 2
Hn. 1, 2 in A
Tpt. 1, 2 in D
A. Trb.
T. Trb.
B. Trb.
Timp.
Vn. 1
Vn. 2
Va.
Vc.
Cb.

7
Fl. 1, 2
a 2
[1]
Ob. 1, 2
a 2
[1]
Cl. 1, 2
in A
Bn. 1, 2
[1]
Hn. 1, 2
in A
Tpt. 1, 2
in D
A. Trb.
T. Trb.
B. Trb.
Timp.
Vn. 1
Vn. 2
Va.
Vc.
Cb.

10
[1]
Fl. 1, 2
[1]
Ob. 1, 2
Cl. 1, 2
in A
[1]
Bn. 1, 2
Hn. 1, 2
in A
Tpt. 1, 2
in D
A. Trb.
T. Trb.
B. Trb.
Timp.
Vn. 1
Vn. 2
Va.
Vc.
Cb.

14
[a 2]
Fl. 1, 2
[a 2]
Ob. 1, 2
Cl. 1, 2 in A
[a 2]
Bn. 1, 2
Hn. 1, 2 in A
Tpt. 1, 2 in D
A. Trb.
T. Trb.
B. Trb.
Timp.
Vn. 1
Vn. 2
Va.
Vc.
Cb.

18
[a 2]
[a 2]
Fl. 1, 2
Ob. 1, 2
Cl. 1, 2 in A
Bn. 1, 2
Hn. 1, 2 in A
Tpt. 1, 2 in D
A. Trb.
T. Trb.
B. Trb.
Timp.
Vn. 1
Vn. 2
Va.
Vc.
Cb.

21
Fl. 1, 2
sf
sf
sf
sf
a 2
Ob. 1, 2
sf
sf
sf
sf
a 2
Cl. 1, 2
in A
Bn. 1, 2
a 2
Hn. 1, 2
in A
a 2
Tpt. 1, 2
in D
A. Trb.
T. Trb.
B. Trb.
Timp.
Vn. 1
sf
sf
sf
sf
Vn. 2
Va.
Vc.
Cb.

25
a 2
Fl. 1, 2
Ob. 1, 2
Cl. 1, 2
in A
Bn. 1, 2
Hn. 1, 2
in A
Tpt. 1, 2
in D
A. Trb.
T. Trb.
B. Trb.
tr
Timp.
Vn. 1
Vn. 2
Va.
Vc.
Cb.

28
Fl. 1, 2
Ob. 1, 2
Cl. 1, 2
in A
a 2
Bn. 1, 2
Hn. 1, 2
in A
Tpt. 1, 2
in D
A. Trb.
T. Trb.
B. Trb.
Timp.
Vn. 1
Vn. 2
Va.
Vc.
Cb.

31
Fl. 1, 2
Ob. 1, 2
Cl. 1, 2
in A
Bn. 1, 2
Hn. 1, 2
in A
Tpt. 1, 2
in D
A. Trb.
T. Trb.
B. Trb.
Timp.
Vn. 1
Vn. 2
Va.
Vc.
Cb.
dim.

287

A
37
Fl. 1, 2
Ob. 1, 2
Cl. 1, 2
in A
Bn. 1, 2
Hn. 1, 2
in A
Tpt. 1, 2
in D
A. Trb.
T. Trb.
B. Trb.
Timp.
Vn. 1
mp
Vn. 2
mp
Va.
mp
Vc.
mp
Cb.
mp

41
Fl. 1, 2
Ob. 1, 2
Cl. 1, 2 in A
Bn. 1, 2
Hn. 1, 2 in A
p
Tpt. 1, 2 in D
p
A. Trb.
T. Trb.
B. Trb.
Timp.
Vn. 1
Vn. 2
Va.
3
3
Vc.
Cb.

45
[1]
Fl. 1, 2
Ob. 1, 2
Cl. 1, 2
in A
Bn. 1, 2
Hn. 1, 2
in A
Tpt. 1, 2
in D
A. Trb.
T. Trb.
B. Trb.
Timp.
Vn. 1
Vn. 2
Va.
Vc.
Cb.
p

49
[1]
Fl. 1, 2
Ob. 1, 2
Cl. 1, 2 in A
1
p
Bn. 1, 2
Hn. 1, 2 in A
Tpt. 1, 2 in D
A. Trb. T. Trb.
B. Trb.
Timp.
Vn. 1
Vn. 2
Va.
Vc.
Cb.

53
[1]
Fl. 1, 2
a 2
Ob. 1, 2
Cl. 1, 2 in A
Bn. 1, 2
Hn. 1, 2 in A
Tpt. 1, 2 in D
A. Trb.
T. Trb.
B. Trb.
Timp.
Vn. 1
Vn. 2
Va.
Vc.
Cb.

57
Fl. 1, 2
Ob. 1, 2
Cl. 1, 2
in A
Bn. 1, 2
Hn. 1, 2
in A
a 2
Tpt. 1, 2
in D
A. Trb.
T. Trb.
B. Trb.
Timp.
Vn. 1
Vn. 2
Va.
Vc.
Cb.
ff
f

60
a 2
Fl. 1, 2
a 2
Ob. 1, 2
Cl. 1, 2
in A
Bn. 1, 2
a 2
Hn. 1, 2
in A
Tpt. 1, 2
in D
A. Trb.
T. Trb.
B. Trb.
Timp.
Vn. 1
Vn. 2
Va.
Vc.
Cb.

295

66
[a 2]
[a 2]
[a 2]
Fl. 1, 2
Ob. 1, 2
Cl. 1, 2
in A
Bn. 1, 2
Hn. 1, 2
in A
Tpt. 1, 2
in D
A. Trb.
T. Trb.
B. Trb.
Timp.
Vn. 1
Vn. 2
Va.
Vc.
Cb.

69
2.
a 2
Fl. 1, 2
Ob. 1, 2
Cl. 1, 2
in A
Bn. 1, 2
Hn. 1, 2
in A
Tpt. 1, 2
in D
A. Trb.
T. Trb.
B. Trb.
Timp.
2.
Vn. 1
Vn. 2
Va.
Vc.
Cb.

298

B
77
Fl. 1, 2
Ob. 1, 2
Cl. 1, 2 in A
Bn. 1, 2
Hn. 1, 2 in A
Tpt. 1, 2 in D
A. Trb. T. Trb.
B. Trb.
Timp.
Vn. 1
Vn. 2
Va.
Vc.
Cb.

82
Vn. 1
Vn. 2
Va.
Vc.
Cb.
86
Fl. 1, 2
Ob. 1, 2
Bn. 1, 2
Vn. 1
Vn. 2
Va.
Vc.
Cb.
a 2
a 2
p
p
f
cresc.

89
Fl. 1, 2
a 2
ff
Ob. 1, 2
a 2
ff
Cl. 1, 2 in A
[cresc.]
ff
Bn. 1, 2
ff
Hn. 1, 2 in A
Tpt. 1, 2 in D
A. Trb.
T. Trb.
ff
B. Trb.
ff
Timp.
Vn. 1
ff
Vn. 2
ff
Va.
ff
Vc.
ff
Cb.
ff

93
1
[a 2]
Fl. 1, 2
p
ff
1
Ob. 1, 2
p
ff
Cl. 1, 2
in A
p
[♯]
[𝄽]
ff
Bn. 1, 2
p
ff
Hn. 1, 2
in A
Tpt. 1, 2
in D
ff
A. Trb.
T. Trb.
ff
B. Trb.
ff
Timp.
Vn. 1
ff
Vn. 2
p
ff
Va.
p
ff
Vc.
p
ff
Cb.
p
ff

97
Fl. 1, 2
1
p
Ob. 1, 2
1
p
Cl. 1, 2
in A
p
p
Bn. 1, 2
p
p
Hn. 1, 2
in A
a 2
ff
Tpt. 1, 2
in D
A. Trb.
T. Trb.
B. Trb.
Timp.
Vn. 1
p
Vn. 2
p
Va.
p
Vc.
p
Cb.
p

101
[a 2]
Fl. 1, 2
ff
[a 2]
Ob. 1, 2
ff
Cl. 1, 2
in A
ff
Bn. 1, 2
ff
Hn. 1, 2
in A
ff
Tpt. 1, 2
in D
ff
A. Trb.
T. Trb.
ff
B. Trb.
ff
Timp.
Vn. 1
ff
Vn. 2
ff
Va.
ff
Vc.
ff
Cb.
ff

105
Fl. 1, 2
Ob. 1, 2
Cl. 1, 2 in A
Bn. 1, 2
Hn. 1, 2 in A
Tpt. 1, 2 in D
A. Trb.
T. Trb.
B. Trb.
Timp.
ff
Vn. 1
Vn. 2
Va.
Vc.
Cb.

C
108
Fl. 1, 2
a 2
ff
Ob. 1, 2
a 2
Cl. 1, 2
in A
Bn. 1, 2
Hn. 1, 2
in A
Tpt. 1, 2
in D
A. Trb.
T. Trb.
B. Trb.
Timp.
Vn. 1
Vn. 2
Va.
Vc.
Cb.

*See Critical Notes.

115
Fl. 1, 2
a 2
p
Ob. 1, 2
a 2
p
Cl. 1, 2
in A
a 2
p
Bn. 1, 2
a 2
p
Hn. 1, 2
in A
p
Tpt. 1, 2
in D
a 2
p
A. Trb.
T. Trb.
p
B. Trb.
p
Timp.
Vn. 1
p
Vn. 2
p
Va.
p
Vc.
p
Cb.
p

309

121
[a 2]
[a 2]
a 2
[a 2]
Fl. 1, 2
Ob. 1, 2
Cl. 1, 2 in A
Bn. 1, 2
Hn. 1, 2 in A
Tpt. 1, 2 in D
A. Trb.
T. Trb.
B. Trb.
Timp.
Vn. 1
Vn. 2
Va.
Vc.
Cb.
tr
ff

125
[a 2]
a 2
Fl. 1, 2
Ob. 1, 2
Cl. 1, 2 in A
Bn. 1, 2
Hn. 1, 2 in A
Tpt. 1, 2 in D
A. Trb.
T. Trb.
B. Trb.
Timp.
Vn. 1
Vn. 2
Va.
Vc.
Cb.

128
Fl. 1, 2
a 2
Ob. 1, 2
a 2
[a 2]
Cl. 1, 2
in A
Bn. 1, 2
Hn. 1, 2
in A
Tpt. 1, 2
in D
A. Trb.
T. Trb.
B. Trb.
Timp.
Vn. 1
Vn. 2
Va.
Vc.
Cb.

131
Fl. 1, 2
[1]
Ob. 1, 2
[1]
Cl. 1, 2 in A
Bn. 1, 2
a 2
Hn. 1, 2 in A
Tpt. 1, 2 in D
A. Trb. T. Trb.
B. Trb.
Timp.
Vn. 1
Vn. 2
Va.
Vc.
Cb.

314

137
[a 2]
Fl. 1, 2
[a 2]
Ob. 1, 2
Cl. 1, 2 in A
Bn. 1, 2
Hn. 1, 2 in A
Tpt. 1, 2 in D
A. Trb.
T. Trb.
B. Trb.
Timp.
Vn. 1
Vn. 2
Va.
Vc.
Cb.

140
[a 2]
Fl. 1, 2
[a 2]
Ob. 1, 2
a 2
Cl. 1, 2
in A
a 2
Bn. 1, 2
Hn. 1, 2
in A
[a 2]
Tpt. 1, 2
in D
A. Trb.
T. Trb.
B. Trb.
Timp.
Vn. 1
Vn. 2
Va.
Vc.
Cb.

317

D
147
[a 2]
Fl. 1, 2
a 2
Ob. 1, 2
a 2
a 2
Cl. 1, 2 in A
a 2
Bn. 1, 2
[1]
Hn. 1, 2 in A
Tpt. 1, 2 in D
A. Trb. T. Trb.
B. Trb.
tr
Timp.
Vn. 1
Vn. 2
Va.
Vc.
Cb.

150
Fl. 1, 2
Ob. 1, 2
Cl. 1, 2
in A
Bn. 1, 2
Hn. 1, 2
in A
Tpt. 1, 2
in D
A. Trb.
T. Trb.
B. Trb.
Timp.
Vn. 1
Vn. 2
Va.
Vc.
Cb.

153
Fl. 1, 2
Ob. 1, 2
Cl. 1, 2
in A
Bn. 1, 2
Hn. 1, 2
in A
Tpt. 1, 2
in D
a 2
A. Trb.
T. Trb.
B. Trb.
Timp.
Vn. 1
Vn. 2
Va.
Vc.
Cb.

321

160
a 2
Fl. 1, 2
a 2
Ob. 1, 2
Cl. 1, 2
in A
Bn. 1, 2
Hn. 1, 2
in A
Tpt. 1, 2
in D
A. Trb.
T. Trb.
B. Trb.
Timp.
Vn. 1
Vn. 2
Va.
3
3
Vc.
Cb.

E
164
[1]
Fl. 1, 2
Ob. 1, 2
Cl. 1, 2
in A
Bn. 1, 2
Hn. 1, 2
in A
Tpt. 1, 2
in D
a 2
mp
A. Trb.
T. Trb.
mp
B. Trb.
mp
Timp.
Vn. 1
Vn. 2
Va.
Vc.
Cb.

168
[1]
Fl. 1, 2
Ob. 1, 2
1
Cl. 1, 2 in A
1
Bn. 1, 2
Hn. 1, 2 in A
Tpt. 1, 2 in D
a 2
A. Trb.
T. Trb.
B. Trb.
Timp.
Vn. 1
Vn. 2
Va.
Vc.
Cb.

172
Fl. 1, 2
Ob. 1, 2
[a 2]
Cl. 1, 2 in A
Bn. 1, 2
[1]
Hn. 1, 2 in A
a 2
Tpt. 1, 2 in D
A. Trb. T. Trb.
B. Trb.
Timp.
Vn. 1
Vn. 2
Va.
Vc.
Cb.

177
[1]
Fl. 1, 2
[a 2]
Ob. 1, 2
Cl. 1, 2 in A
Bn. 1, 2
a 2
Hn. 1, 2 in A
Tpt. 1, 2 in D
A. Trb.
T. Trb.
B. Trb.
Timp.
Vn. 1
Vn. 2
Va.
Vc.
Cb.

180
Fl. 1, 2
Ob. 1, 2
Cl. 1, 2
in A
Bn. 1, 2
a 2
Hn. 1, 2
in A
Tpt. 1, 2
in D
A. Trb.
T. Trb.
B. Trb.
Timp.
Vn. 1
Vn. 2
Va.
Vc.
Cb.

183
Fl. 1, 2
Ob. 1, 2
Cl. 1, 2
in A
a 2
Bn. 1, 2
Hn. 1, 2
in A
Tpt. 1, 2
in D
A. Trb.
T. Trb.
B. Trb.
Timp.
Vn. 1
Vn. 2
Va.
Vc.
Cb.

186
a 2
Fl. 1, 2
Ob. 1, 2
Cl. 1, 2
in A
[2]
Bn. 1, 2
p
Hn. 1, 2
in A
p
Tpt. 1, 2
in D
p
A. Trb.
T. Trb.
B. Trb.
tr
Timp.
p
Vn. 1
p
Vn. 2
p
Va.
p
Vc.
p
Cb.
p

191
Fl. 1, 2
solo
p
Ob. 1, 2
solo
p
Cl. 1, 2
in A
Bn. 1, 2
[2]
p
Hn. 1, 2
in A
Tpt. 1, 2
in D
A. Trb.
T. Trb.
B. Trb.
Timp.
Vn. 1
Vn. 2
Va.
Vc.
Cb.

196
Fl. 1, 2
Ob. 1, 2
Cl. 1, 2
in A
p
Bn. 1, 2
Hn. 1, 2
in A
Tpt. 1, 2
in D
A. Trb.
T. Trb.
p
B. Trb.
p
Timp.
Vn. 1
Vn. 2
Va.
Vc.
Cb.

F
200
Fl. 1, 2
Ob. 1, 2
Cl. 1, 2 in A
Bn. 1, 2
Hn. 1, 2 in A
Tpt. 1, 2 in D
A. Trb.
T. Trb.
B. Trb.
Timp.
Vn. 1
Vn. 2
Va.
Vc.
Cb.
[1]
p

203
Fl. 1, 2
Ob. 1, 2
Cl. 1, 2
in A
Bn. 1, 2
Hn. 1, 2
in A
Tpt. 1, 2
in D
A. Trb.
T. Trb.
B. Trb.
Timp.
Vn. 1
Vn. 2
Va.
Vc.
Cb.

206
[1]
Fl. 1, 2
p
Ob. 1, 2
Cl. 1, 2
in A
[1]
p
Bn. 1, 2
[1]
Hn. 1, 2
in A
a 2
p
Tpt. 1, 2
in D
[1]
p
A. Trb.
T. Trb.
B. Trb.
Timp.
Vn. 1
Vn. 2
Va.
p
Vc.
p
Cb.
p

210
Fl. 1, 2
cresc.
f
Ob. 1, 2
[1]
[cresc.]
f
Cl. 1, 2 in A
cresc.
f
Bn. 1, 2
cresc.
f
Hn. 1, 2 in A
[cresc.]
f
Tpt. 1, 2 in D
f
A. Trb.
T. Trb.
B. Trb.
Timp.
tr
f
Vn. 1
f
Vn. 2
f
Va.
cresc.
f
Vc.
cresc.
f
Cb.
cresc.
f

214
Fl. 1, 2
Ob. 1, 2
Cl. 1, 2
in A
Bn. 1, 2
Hn. 1, 2
in A
Tpt. 1, 2
in D
A. Trb.
T. Trb.
f
B. Trb.
f
Timp.
Vn. 1
Vn. 2
Va.
Vc.
Cb.

218
Fl. 1, 2
a 2
p
Ob. 1, 2
a 2
p
Cl. 1, 2
in A
a 2
Bn. 1, 2
a 2
p
Hn. 1, 2
in A
p
Tpt. 1, 2
in D
A. Trb.
T. Trb.
B. Trb.
Timp.
Vn. 1
p
Vn. 2
p
Va.
p
Vc.
p
Cb.
p

222
a 2
G
Fl. 1, 2
a 2
Ob. 1, 2
Cl. 1, 2
in A
p
Bn. 1, 2
Hn. 1, 2
in A
Tpt. 1, 2
in D
A. Trb.
T. Trb.
B. Trb.
Timp.
Vn. 1
Vn. 2
Va.
Vc.
Cb.
f

339

230
[a 2]
Fl. 1, 2
ff
Ob. 1, 2
[a 2]
[a 2]
Cl. 1, 2 in A
[a 2]
Bn. 1, 2
[a 2]
Hn. 1, 2 in A
Tpt. 1, 2 in D
A. Trb.
T. Trb.
B. Trb.
Timp.
Vn. 1
Vn. 2
Va.
Vc.
Cb.

234
Fl. 1, 2
Ob. 1, 2
Cl. 1, 2
in A
[a 2]
Bn. 1, 2
a 2
Hn. 1, 2
in A
Tpt. 1, 2
in D
A. Trb.
T. Trb.
B. Trb.
Timp.
Vn. 1
Vn. 2
Va.
Vc.
Cb.

237
[a 2]
Fl. 1, 2
Ob. 1, 2
[a 2]
Cl. 1, 2
in A
[a 2]
Bn. 1, 2
a 2
Hn. 1, 2
in A
Tpt. 1, 2
in D
A. Trb.
T. Trb.
B. Trb.
Timp.
Vn. 1
Vn. 2
Va.
Vc.
Cb.

343

344

Critical Report

Sources

The collection of Alice Mary Smith manuscripts, with some of her printed music, was handed down to her grandson, Rev. Humphrey Kempe, a distinguished amateur musician. On his death the manuscripts were willed to his god-daughter, who gave them to the present editor in order to sort and catalogue. The collection has now been given to the Royal Academy of Music, London, where it is housed in the library.[1]

The Symphony in C Minor consists of one manuscript full score, with a set of parts in another hand, presumably made by a copyist for the 1863 performance by the Musical Society of London. The Symphony in A Minor exists in full score only. Each are in brown paper covers. The cover of the C-minor work is headed: "Symphony in C minor | Alice Mary Smith"; it has 145 pages with one ruled system per page. On page 1 below the title and composer is the detail: "(Tried by the Mus: Soc: of London Nov: 4th 1863)". The orchestral parts have separate books for violin 1, violin 2, viola, bass trombone, and timpani; the remaining wind and brass part books, as well as violoncello and double bass, have the two instruments in each system. The cover of the A-minor work is headed: "Symphony in A minor | By | Σ", and each individual movement is likewise headed with the sigma letter (see plate 4). After her death her husband has written on the front cover:

> A. M. W. Written for, but not sent in in time, & so did not compete for the prize offered for a symphony by the Alex^{ra} Palace C^n. when F. Davenport was first, C. V. Stanford 2nd, Miss O. Prescott 3rd. [The next line is not decipherable.]
>
> F. M. W. 13.1.85.

There are ninety-nine pages of one ruled system per page.

The instrument names in the full scores are in Italian, as follows at the start of each work. Symphony in C Minor: Flauti, Oboi, Clar^{tti} B♭, Fagotti, Corni E♭, Trombe, Trombone Alto, Tenore, Bass, Tympani, Viol 1mo,———2^{ndo}, Viola, Vcello, Basso. Symphony in A Minor: Flauti, Oboi, Clar^{tti} A, Fagotti, Corni C, Trombe D, Tromboni Alto, Tenore, Basso, Timpani A.E., Viol 1mo, Viol 2do, Viola, Vcello, Basso. Key signatures are omitted after the first page of each movement, otherwise the notation of the source scores generally accords with modern convention.

Editorial Methods

The full scores of the symphonies have been the primary sources for this edition, the orchestral parts of the C-minor symphony having been used to confirm details such as wind and brass voicings and expression marks, which are not always clear in the score of this work. The few places where the parts, rather than the full score, have been followed are stated in the critical notes.

Movement numbers have been added editorially for both symphonies; in the A-minor symphony, rehearsal letters are added, as are the "Minuetto" and "Trio" indications in the third movement. Original rehearsal letters, to be found in score and parts of the C-minor symphony (which omit J and K), have been retained. The standard score order in the original has been maintained. Italian instrument names and abbreviations have been given in English. In the C-minor symphony the trombones are written on separate staves using alto, tenor, and bass clefs. In the A-minor work, alto and tenor trombones share a staff in the alto clef. Otherwise clefs are as in the sources, apart from occasional changes in bassoon, viola, and cello parts in order to reduce the number of ledger lines. Timpani parts do not use key signatures in the sources; the edition adds signatures and places tuning indications (according to the convention "in C-G") above the staff at the start of each movement. Tempo and other directives, above the top staff in the sources, have been reproduced above the first violin part. Double barlines (thin-thin), placed at the start of all first time endings in the sources, have been replaced by single barlines.

Beaming patterns of three beamed eighth notes in $\frac{3}{4}$ time have been modernized, otherwise the original patterns have been retained, except where the sources are inconsistent. Stem directions for winds, combined on a single staff in the source scores, are often irrational and have been standardized. The random use of single stemming and opposite stemming in the winds has been rationalized to use single stemming (and single slurs) where possible. In the C-minor symphony the manuscript parts have clarified whether the instruments are solo or are both playing in unison, but voicings are less clear in the A-minor symphony, where editorial voicing suggestions in brackets are more frequent. Only once, on a whole note, is "a 2" indicated, written as "a due" in the score (C-minor symphony, fourth movement, m. 28).

Where unison double stemming is used, or the parts clarify that both instruments play, "a 2" has been added. Voicing indications are tacitly repeated when a line continues over a page turn of the edition. Whole measure rests, left blank in the score, have been filled. Any missing rests, where confirmed in the parts, have been tacitly inserted. Single/opposite stemming and slurring in the strings has been left as in the sources, as it is assumed that the composer intended single stemmed chords to be double-stopped. (Performers may decide that "divisi" may be more appropriate in some places.)

In the C-minor symphony, the double bass line, written for a three-stringed bass (tuned A_1-D-G), has higher octave transpositions in places where the passages that double the cello lie below its lowest string. Such numerous places have been tacitly transposed to the same written notes as the cello to allow for performance on a normal four-stringed instrument with its lowest string tuned to E_1. In the few places where there is doubt, the editorial lower transposition is given as a cue-sized note. (The A-minor symphony is clearly written for the standard four-stringed bass.)

The notation of grace notes has been retained but slurs to the main note, absent in the sources, have been added. Notated appoggiaturas are generally assumed to be performed as acciaccaturas. All tremolos taken to be measured and all other shorthand conventions, used frequently in the sources, have been notated in full; the tremolos that are assumed to be unmeasured in the second movement of the A-minor symphony (see mm. 158–80) have been left as in the source score in the whole of this passage. In the sources, triplets are always written with a slur and the number on the note side; the number has been moved to the beam side and the slur only retained where the passage would imply slurring. Where the triplet number is missing, this has been added for the first one or two patterns of a passage. A triplet bracket has been used where the group starts with a rest or is unbeamed.

Dynamic and other expression marks are not always written on every staff to which they apply in the source scores. They are often written above an instrumental section, where they are assumed to apply to the whole section and have therefore been placed below each staff of that section without comment, except where there is an element of doubt as to whether they apply to all instruments of that section, when the editorial conventions (as set out below) have been used. Sometimes a single expression mark is written between two staves (see plate 3) and this has likewise been reproduced below the appropriate staves. Editorial dynamics are in bold type. In the C-minor symphony, where the dynamics occur in the parts but not in the score, these are shown in non-bold italics in parentheses. Editorial hairpins are dashed; hairpins in the parts but not in the score are in parentheses. Accents, written < in the sources, have been modernized to >. Editorial accents and other articulations are in square brackets; those considered necessary to match other places, and found in the parts only, have been added in parentheses. The parts have many additional accents that do not appear in the score; these have been ignored, except where noted.

Slurs missing from some instruments in the source scores have been added without comment in the C-minor symphony only when confirmed by the parts. Editorial slurs and ties are dashed; those found only in the parts and not in the score are dotted. The slurring to be found in these works is not always clear; often a slur will extend over a whole measure, and even overlap into the next measure (see plate 3, m. 4), where bowing slurs and phrase marks may become confused. Where there is a clear confusion (and where it is not resolved by the parts) the phrase mark has been deleted and a critical note has been given. In the edition the positioning of slur ends has been altered to align with the appropriate notehead. The sources sometimes use converging slurs, which have generally been combined into a single slur. Although a slur does not enclose a tie in the sources, slurs have been drawn to enclose the ties, even when several ties are present. Repeated notes which are slurred in the strings, intended as bowing slurs, have been left as in the source (see C-minor symphony, first movement, mm. 152, 203, 446; third movement, mm. 104, 114; A-minor symphony, first movement, mm. 180, 194). In the timpani part, a continuous roll over several measures often omits ties, although in some cases they are present; the source notation has been followed in either case.

Editorial accidentals are in brackets; added cautionary accidentals are in parentheses. Occasional redundant accidentals and unnecessary cautionaries have been tacitly removed. Occasional missing accidentals in the C-minor symphony, where confirmed in the parts, have been added tacitly. Accidentals on a tied note repeated on each measure have also been tacitly removed.

Critical Notes

These notes report differences between the sources and the edition that are not covered by editorial methods above. Abbreviations of cited parts are as follows: Fl. = Flute; Ob. = Oboe; Cl. = Clarinet; Bn. = Bassoon; Hn. = Horn; Tpt. = Trumpet; Trb. = Trombone (with Alto, Tenor, and Bass indicated as 1, 2, and 3); Timp. = Timpani; Vn. = Violin; Va. = Viola; Vc. = Violoncello; Cb. = Contrabass. Str. = strings; Ww. = woodwinds. In reports of paired instruments sharing a single staff, the instruments are specified as, for instance, "Fl. 1," "Fl. 2," or "Fl. 1-2" according to how they are presented in this edition, even if the designations are editorial. Notes, including grace notes, are numbered consecutively through a measure; notes sounding simultaneously are numbered from bottom to top. Where appropriate, chords or beats are numbered rather than specific notes. Pitch references are indicated using the system where middle C = c'.

Symphony in C Minor (1863)

In this work, the abbreviation sc. refers to the primary source, the manuscript full score; pt(s). refers to the manuscript set of orchestral parts. It is assumed that the markings in red pencil referred to in the notes below were added during rehearsals for the 1863 trial performance. The key of the trumpets, not specified in the score, is incorrectly noted in the part as "in E♭" for movements I and III, but "in C" for movement IV. The part is written for trumpets in C throughout. The tuning of the timpani is specified only in movement IV.

I. Grave; Allegro ma non troppo

Mm. 1–2, Vn. 1 has chords g' + c" (m. 1) and f' + c" (m. 2), with the upper notes lightly scratched out; m. 1, Vn. 2 has chord c' + e', with upper note scratched out—these upper notes have been eradicated in most pts. M. 1, Bn. 1, Va., and Vc. have phrase slur from note 1 to m. 4, note 1; m. 8, from note 2 to m. 12, note 1. M. 41, Ob. 1 and Bn. 1 have slur from note 2 to m. 42, note 1. M. 50, sc. has rehearsal letter A; moved to m. 49 to accord with pts. M. 97, Vn. 1, notes have accents; deleted to match other parts. Mm. 109–10, Hn. 1-2, notes are g'. Mm. 146–48, Vn. 2, notes 1–3 are slurred in sc.; notes 1–2 slurred in accord with pts. Mm. 161–64, Cl. 1, notes 1–3 are slurred in sc.; notes 1–2 slurred in accord with pt. M. 198, Vn. 2 is marked *cresc*. Mm. 203–8, Vn. 1 and Vn. 2, and mm. 203–4, Cb. have slurs both over two quarter notes in each measure and over four notes in two measures; paired slurs have been deleted to accord with m. 513ff. M. 212, Ob. 1, sc. is marked "solo". M. 235, Cb., note 1 is up an octave. M. 249, Vn. 2, notes have staccato dots. M. 294, Cl. 1-2, note 2 has ♮ in sc. and pts. Mm. 297–98, Cb. has rests. M. 306, Ob. 1, note 1 has *p*; moved as shown in edition. M. 317, Bn. 2, beat 2 is quarter note in pt.; and m. 318 is given to Bn. 1 in pt. M. 386, Str. have *p* in sc. M. 390, Ob. 1-2, sc. and pt. have *p*. M. 436, Vn. 1, note 1 has *f*. M. 459, Vn. 1, slur extends to m. 460, note 1 in sc. and pts.; altered to accord with mm. 149–50. M. 479, Fl. 1-2, slur extends to chord in m. 480. Mm. 480–82, Ob. 1 line in edition is *a 2* in pt. M. 481, Vn. 1, Vn. 2, and Va. have additional slur from note 2 to m. 482, note 1, and from m. 482, note 2 to m. 483, note 1, additional slurs deleted to accord with mm. 170–73. M. 482, Cl. 1-2 and Bn. 1-2, slur extends from chord 2 to chord 4; altered to accord with string parts. Mm. 501–2, Bn. 1 and Hn. 1 have slur in each measure in pts. M. 522, Ob. 1, sc. is marked "solo". M. 543, Fl. 1-2 has *sf* in sc.; other Ww. marked *pp* in pts. M. 544, rehearsal letter added editorially. M. 551, Timp. marked *f* in pt. Mm. 552 and 556, sc. and pts. have *p* added in red pencil in m. 552 and *cresc.* in m. 556 (both included in edition) with dashes through to m. 572. M. 558, Fl. 1-2 has *p*, Cl. 1-2 has *f* added in red pencil in pts. M. 564, Trb. 1-3 marked *ff* in pts.

II. Allegretto amorevole

M. 12, Vn. 2 has slur on notes 1–2. M. 15, Va. and Vc., note 1 has *pp* in pts. M. 16, Vn. 1, sc. has slur from note to m. 17, note 1; crossed through in pts. M. 19, Vn. 1, slur extends from note 1 to note 6 in pt. Mm. 21–22, Hn. 2 is eradicated in pt. Mm. 27, 28, 30, Vn. 2, and mm. 28, 30, 33, Va. have slurs on notes 1–5 in sc.; edition altered to accord with pts. M. 54, Vn. 1 and Vn. 2, note 1 has *pp* in pts. M. 61, Vc. has slur extending to note 2, with separate slur in m. 62 on notes 1–3; altered to match edition's reading for Vn. 1. M. 64, Cb. has slur on notes 2–3. M. 72, Cl. 1, note 1 has *cresc.* in pt. M. 85, Hn. 1, note 1 has *p* in pt. Mm. 88 and 90, Cl. 2, note 2 is a♭'; mm. 89, 91, and 92, Cl. 2, note 1 is a♭'. Mm. 96 and 158, Cl. 2 has notes 4–5 as in Cl. 1 in pt. (i.e., *a 2*), but sc. has stems up indicating Cl. 1 only. M. 98, Vn. 1, note 1 has accent in sc. Mm. 139–40, Fl. 1, and m. 143, Cl. 1 and Va. have *tr* sign repeated on each note. M. 142, Va. has *pp* in pt. Mm. 150 and 152, Cl. 2, note 3 is a♭'; m. 154, Cl. 2, note 1 is a♭'. M. 153, Bn. 1 and Hn. 1-2 have dotted quarter note in pts.

III. Allegro ma non troppo

All appoggiaturas are left as in sc., but with slur added; the pts. generally alter these to acciaccaturas. Mm. 1–3, Cb. left as in sc., as lower octave would have been possible on three-stringed bass. M. 2, Vn. 1 and Vn. 2 have *f* on note 1; removed as redundant. Mm. 19 and 27, Cl. 2, note 1 is a♭'. M. 120, Str. have *ff*; moved as shown in edition. M. 128, Vn. 1 and Vn. 2, note 1 has *f* in pts. M. 131, Vn. 1, note 1 has accent. M. 153, Str. have *mf* on note 1; moved as shown in edition. M. 168, Bn. 1-2, beat 1 has *p* in pt. Mm. 170–72, Trb. 2 has ties in pt., which have been eradicated; the slur of edition is found in both sc. and pt. M. 210, Vn. 2, and m. 212, Vn. 1, note 1 has *sf* in pt. Mm. 210–11, Hn. 1-2, notes are d" in sc., with added ♯ in pt. M. 239, Ob. 1, note 1 is f" in pt. M. 245 has *sempre ff* above system, moved in Ww. as shown in edition. M. 264 has "accell:" pencilled into sc. and added in pts. M. 303, Vn. 2, note 2 is a♭'; altered to accord with Vn. 1.

IV. Allegro maestoso

In the full score the clarinets have the key signature for B♭ instruments but are written in C, while in the manuscript part they are headed "in C"; B♭ clarinets have been retained in the edition and the music transposed accordingly. M. 1, accents are written only for flutes, but have been added to all instruments, as in pts. Mm. 7, 102, and 225, Cb., beat 2 is triplet quarter note *g* followed by 8th note B. M. 13, Str., pts. have crescendo hairpin from beat 3 to end of m. 14. M. 16, Va., note 3 has *p* in pts. M. 18, Fl. 1 and Ob. 1, slur extends from note 1 to note 6. Mm. 25 and 29, Vn. 1 has *p* on note 1; moved as shown in edition. M. 65, Va. and Vc., note 1 has *pp* in pts. M. 70, Ob. 1, note is a♯". M. 72, Fl. 1 has rests missing in sc.; pt. has quarter note with rests. Mm. 73–74, 209–10, 271, Vc., and mm. 73–74 and 271, Cb. have staccato dots on notes 1–2 in pts. M. 74–76, the hairpins are added in red pencil in both sc. and pts. M. 78, Vn. 1 and Vn. 2 have crescendo hairpin in red pencil in pts. only from note 3 to m. 79, note 1, and decrescendo hairpin from m. 79, note 3 to m. 80, note 1. Mm. 78–79, Vc. and Cb., the continuation of half notes with two measured tremolo slashes (i.e., repeated 16th notes) may be intended in these measures. M. 79, Va., notes 18–20 have staccato dots under slur in some pts. Mm. 82 and 84, Fl. 1, Ob. 1, and Bn. 1 have slur from note 2 in pts. M. 85, Vn. 2, Va., and Vc./Cb. pts. have crescendo hairpin from note 1 to end of m. 87. M. 87, Vn. 1, notes 5–8 have staccato dots in pts. M. 92, Str., pts. have crescendo hairpin from beat 3. M. 108, Vn. 1 and Vn. 2, pts. have crescendo hairpin from note 3 to m. 109, note 4. M. 112, Vn. 1 has *mf* on note 1; altered to *p* and moved to m. 111 (as mm. 25 and 29, see above). Mm. 144–45, Vn. 1 and Va. have slur over each triplet in sc.; as shown in edition in pts. M. 159, Vn. 1, note 1 has *ff* in pts. M. 210, Vn. 1 has staccato dots from note 3 to m. 211, note 8 in pts; m. 211, Vn. 2 has staccato dots in pts. M. 234, Vn. 1 has *dim.* on note 2 in pts.; altered in edition to accord with mm. 24, 28, and 111. M. 248, Vn. 2 has slur on notes 5–8 in sc.; Va. has slur on notes 6–8 in pts. M. 268, Ww. have *psf* in sc. M. 275, Vn. 1, pts. only have crescendo hairpin from note 2 to m. 276, note 6, and decrescendo hairpin from m. 277, note 5 to note in m. 278. M. 280, Va., sc. and pts. are notated as half-note dyad with two measured tremolo slashes; altered as shown in edition. Mm. 292–94, Vn. 1, Vn. 2, and Va., pts. show slurring of triplets as shown in edition; sc. has triplet "3" and slur over notes (see editorial methods). M. 301, Timp., trill line is continuous to m. 302, note 2. M. 306, Tpt. 1-2, Trb. 1-2, and Trb. 3 are marked *f*. M. 310, Trb. 2-3, pts. have slur and accents from note 1 to m. 313, note 1. M. 312, Bn. 1 and Trb. 2, note 2 is e♭'. M. 324, Ob. 2 and Cl. 2, note 4 is e♭"; Bn. 1 and Trb. 2, note 4 is e♭'; Vn. 2, note 8 is e♭". M. 330, Va., note 9 (lowest note of chord on beat 4) is d'.

Symphony in A Minor (1876)

I. Allegro

Mm. 26 and 34, Vn. 2, Va., Vc., and Cb. have *sf*. M. 28, Cl. 1-2, Bn. 1-2, and Hn. 1 have *p* on beat 1; moved as shown in edition (cf. m. 253). M. 34, Str., *fz* and *sf* (see report for mm. 26 and 34 above) are on beat 1; moved as shown in edition. M. 57, Vn. 1, note 2 is g♯", and Vn. 2, note 2 is g♯'. M. 63, Vn. 1 has *p* on note 1; moved as shown in edition. M. 67, Cl. 1 has two tied quarter notes. M. 94, Vc., slur extends to m. 95, note 2. M. 98, Ob. 2 has two quarter notes. M. 127, Va., note 1 is d♭'; Vc. and Cb., note 1 is d♭. M. 129, Fl. 1 and Ob. 1, notes have stems up, with no rests underneath. M. 150, Ob. 1-2, Hn. 1-2, and Str. (except Cb.) have *f* on beat 1; moved as shown in edition. Mm. 149–61, Fl. 1, notes have stems up, with no rests underneath. M. 157, Va., beat 1 has quarter-note dyad with two measured tremolo slashes, lacking augmentation dot. M. 159, Trb. 1-2 and Trb. 3 have *f*; removed as redundant. M. 165, beat 2 through m. 167, Bn. 1, notes are g♭'. M. 172 through m. 175, note 1, Cl. 2, notes are c". M. 172, note 3 through m. 175, Fl. 1, notes have stems up, with no rests underneath. M. 178, Bn. 2, notes are tied; altered to accord with mm. 164 and 171. M. 179, Fl. 1, note 1 is e♭"; Cl. 1, note 1 is g♭'. M. 179, Vc. and Cb. have *pp* on note 2; moved as shown in edition. Mm. 183 and 185, Vc. and Cb. have slur to note in mm. 184 and 186, respectively. M. 205, Vn. 1 and Vn. 2, note 1 lacks augmentation dot. M. 217, Tpt. 1-2, notes have stems up, with no rest underneath, but bar remains *a 2* in edition. M. 219, Trb. 3, note 1 has ♯. M. 220, Fl. 1, note appears to be d'". Mm. 222–23, Vn. 2, notes have measured tremolo 16th slashes. M. 223, Hn. 1-2, both have slur to m. 224. M. 237, Vn. 1 has *pp* on note 1; moved as shown in edition. M. 273, Fl. 1 has two tied quarter notes. M. 283, Vn. 2, slur extends only to note 4; altered to accord with Vn. 1. M. 311, Vn. 2, note 1 is a'. Mm. 314, 316, and 319–20, Hn. 1-2, notes are c" and c'. M. 321, all parts have *p* on beat 1; moved as shown in edition. M. 335, Timp., trill line extends to note. M. 338, Vn. 1, notes have measured tremolo 16th slashes. M. 343, Cl. 2, note 1 has ♯. M. 346, Tpt. 1-2, beat 1, note values are beamed 16th, 8th, 16th. M. 355, Cl. 2, note 2 has ♯.

II. Andante

Trombone parts are headed "Trb. 1, 2, 3". Mm. 2 and 4, Vn. 1, crescendo and decrescendo hairpins are on note 2; extended in edition to match mm. 105–8. Mm. 2 and 4, Vc. and Cb. appear to have tied dotted-quarter note A's overwritten (making a pedal A throughout mm. 1–5); the original notes have been retained in the edition in line with mm. 31–35 and 104–8. M. 2, Vc. and Cb. have *pp* on note 1; moved as shown in edition. M. 8, Bn. 2, note lacks augmentation dot. M. 15, Cl. 2, note 2 is b'. M. 25, Cl. 1-2, beat 3, note stems for Cl. 1 and 2 are reversed. M. 27, Bn. 2, notes are tied. M. 35, Cb. has slur to note in m. 36. Mm. 39–40 and 43–46, Timp., notes are unbeamed, having separate flags; rolls have been added to note 1 in these measures to accord with later passages. M. 46, Bn. 1 and Cb., slur extends to note 4. M. 55, Vn. 1, slur extends to note 4. M. 56, Vn. 2 has slur to m. 57, note 1. M. 65, Hn. 1-2 and Tpt. 1-2, note 2, [♮] indicates an inflection not possible on the natural horn/trumpet, but suggested for the modern horn/trumpet. Mm. 67–68, Timp., notes are unbeamed, having separate flags. M. 81, Bn. 1-2 has *pp* on beat 1; moved as shown in edition. M. 87, Vc., note lacks augmentation dot. M. 103, Va., slur extends to note 6. M. 113, Va., sc. has measure repeat sign, but note 1 is altered as shown in edition. M. 117, Cl. 1, note 4 is e♮". M. 119, Va., notes 1–2 are 16th notes. M. 120, Ob. 1, ♮ on note 1 appears to be scratched out. M. 122, Fl. 1 has ♮ on note 2; moved to note 1 in edition. M. 143, Fl. 2, Ob. 1-2, and Bn. 2, beat 2 is quarter note. M. 151, Vn. 2, note lacks augmentation dot. M. 153, Vn. 2 and Va., notes lack augmentation dots. M. 156, Vn. 2 and Cb., measure is blank (presumably measure repeat sign was intended). M. 160, Trb. 2, note 2 and Va., note 5 are c♮'. M. 162, Ob. 1-2, chords 2–3 are 8th notes; altered to 16ths in edition. M. 164, Vc. and Cb., notes 2 and 6 have no tremolo slashes. M. 170, Vc., slur extends over the full measure. M. 185, Cb., slur extends over the full measure.

III. Allegretto

Mm. 9–11, Fl. 1-2, Cl. 1-2, and Bn. 1-2, slurs and ties appear partially scratched out; they have been retained to accord with mm. 33–35. M. 9, Vn. 2, notes 3–4 are g'–c'. Mm. 16–17 lack repeat signs and m. 44 lacks backward repeat sign.   M. 38, Fl. 1 and Ob. 1 have slur to m. 39, note 1.   Mm. 49–51, Hn. 1-2, notes are c″ and c′.   M. 62 lacks forward repeat sign and m. 77 lacks backward repeat sign.   M. 68, Bn. 1, notes 1–2 are slurred.   M. 71, Hn. 2 has slur to note in m. 72.   M. 77, Vn. 1, grace notes are before the barline.   M. 78, final double barline has no change of key.

IV. ALLEGRO

Trombone parts are headed "Trb. 1, 2, 3".   Mm. 3 and 126, Va., beat 3, chord is a+e′; altered to accord with mm. 7 and 130.   Mm. 7 and 130, Trb. 2, note 3 is a.   M. 8, beat 4 through m. 14, beat 3, Fl. 1 and Ob. 1, notes have stems up, with no rests underneath.   M. 14, beat 4 through m. 15, Fl. 1-2, notes have stems up, with no rests underneath.   Mm. 9, 10, and 11, Fl. 1 and Ob. 1, notes 1–2 have staccato dots; altered to match Vn. 1.   M. 17, beat 3 through m. 18, Ww. and Vn. 1 have 8th notes followed by 8th rests scratched out and replaced by quarter notes; the edition retains the original in line with mm. 140–41.   M. 23, Cl. 2, note 4 is e″.   Mm. 26 and 149, Timp. has two half notes, with trill line extending throughout the measure.   M. 32, Cl. 1, note 1 has ♯.   M. 36, Cl. 1-2 has two tied half-note dyads, with further ties reaching into m. 37 (which has a measure repeat sign).   M. 55, Va. has two tied half notes.   M. 59, Trb. 3, note 4 is e.   M. 71, Tpt. 1, Trb. 2, and Trb. 3 have slur to note in m. 72.   M. 89, Cl. 2 and Bn. 2 have two tied half notes.   M. 89, Vn. 1, notes 1–3 are f♮″.   M. 106, Trb. 3, and m. 108, Cb., slur extends from note 1 to note 4.   M. 113, Hn. 1-2, beat 3, note 2, [♭] indicates an inflection not possible on the natural horn, but suggested for the modern horn.   M. 116, Fl. 1, Cl. 1, and Trb. 1 have two tied half notes.   M. 117, Tpt. 1-2 has slur on notes 1–2.   M. 128, Vn. 1 and Vn. 2, note 3 is 8th note with 8th rest (Vn. 2 is marked "col Viol 1mo").   M. 126, Vc. and Cb., notes 1–2 are 8th notes followed by 8th rests; altered to accord with m. 3.   M. 130, Vc. and Cb., notes 1–2 are 8th notes followed by 8th rests, and note 3 is quarter note followed by 8th rest; altered to accord with m. 7.   Mm. 131–33, Vn. 1, beat 4 is dotted 8th note followed by 16th note.   Mm. 131 and 134, Vc. and Cb., beat 4 is dotted 8th note followed by 16th note; altered to match mm. 8 and 11.   M. 147, Hn. 1-2 has quarter rest on beat 1.   M. 155, Cl. 1-2 has two tied half-note dyads but lacks further ties (cf. m. 36 above) into m. 156 (which has a measure repeat sign).   M. 170, Vc., slurs on triplets extend to following quarter notes; altered to accord with m. 51.   Mm. 170–71, Vn. 1, Vn. 2, and Cb., slurs on triplets extend to following quarter notes; altered to accord with mm. 51–52.   M. 174, Bn. 2 has two tied half notes.   M. 177, Va., beat 1, upper note of chord is a′.   M. 200, Vn. 1, notes 2–4 are c♯‴ a″ c♯‴, with slash repeat sign for beats 3 and 4.   M. 214, Cb., note 4 is D.   M. 235, Fl. 1-2, note 1 is a″.   M. 247, Vn. 1 and Vn. 2, note 6 lacks ledger line.   M. 248, Timp., note is half note with no rest.

Note

1. On the death of Frederick Meadows White in 1898 the Smith manuscripts and printed music were willed to the elder daughter Ida. Ida (Gay) Meadows White (1868–1950) married Sir Alfred Bray Kempe, F.R.S. (a second marriage) in 1897, becoming Lady Kempe. A lawyer by profession, Sir Alfred was an accomplished musician, a counter-tenor, member of the original Bach Choir, mathematician, alpinist, honorary treasurer and vice-president of The Royal Society, and secretary to the National Antarctic Expedition (1901–4), later having Mount Kempe and the Kempe Glacier named after him. On Ida's death the material became the property of their eldest son, Rev. Alfred Humphrey Meadows Kempe (1900–1988), a choral scholar at King's College Cambridge, who became assistant secretary at the Royal Academy of Music for a short while, later Precentor at Coventry Cathedral, then diocesan secretary at Chichester Cathedral. A keen and perceptive musician, he tried to encourage occasional performances of Smith's works. The "Tubal-Cain" string quartet and the C-minor symphony were tried out in Chichester, the second movement of the symphony being given a public performance by the Chichester Symphony Orchestra conducted by the composer Michael Hurd in 1978. The first movement of the A-minor symphony was tried out by the same orchestra (conducted by the present editor) in 1990. Upon the death of Humphrey Kempe, the manuscripts, together with some copies of Smith's printed music, were left to his god-daughter, Heather Harrison, a professional cellist. The present editor has made a full catalogue of the collection, which differs in a few respects from that listed in *New Grove 2* and *The New Grove Dictionary of Women Composers*.